SAIL
in a
DAY!

SAIL
in a
DAY!

by GEORGE D. O'DAY

with Beverly Harris

GROSSET & DUNLAP

PUBLISHERS   NEW YORK

LIBRARY OF CONGRESS CATALOG CARD NUMBER: 66–11322

ISBN: 0-0448-01540-4

The photograph on the front of the cover is by Howey Caufman. The photograph of the author on the back cover is by Morris Rosenfeld.

PRINTED IN UNITED STATES OF AMERICA

Contents

Anyone, young or old, can learn to sail in a single day. (Courtesy Dorothy Crossley)

Foreword

It is a great temptation if one is familiar with a particular sport to assume that everyone else in the world is also familiar with it. It is an even greater temptation for the knowledgeable to discuss their favorite sport in a manner and language that makes it sound complicated and formidable.

Since this book has been prepared with the newcomer to sailing in mind, I have tried to simplify and limit the technical jargon and have assumed that the largest percentage of readers have only a nodding acquaintance with the sport of sailing.

You may argue that if sailing is so simple to learn, why does it take a hundred pages and pictures to tell us about it? The only explanation to this is that there are many types of beginners to sailing—the individual who only recently has started to become a "guest aboard" a friend's sailboat, the person who just completed a series of "shore school" lessons in sailing at the local YMCA, the father shopping for a sailboat so that he and his son who just learned to sail at camp can take up a sport together, the couple who owned a 14-foot sailcraft and now want to do some cruising in a larger boat for their enlarged family, the powerboat owner who has just traded in his magnificent cruiser for a motor sailer 'cause he's decided its better to join 'em than fight 'em, the wife who is tired of staying home husbandless weekends and has decided to "bone-up" on the sport and make herself useful on her husband's 40 footer, the senior citizen who now has time to enjoy a sport he once was quite active in and needs some review, the landlubber who simply wants to do some armchair sailing—it is all these people and many more I have tried to keep in mind when writing and choosing illustrations for this book.

Nowhere near the complete sailing story can be told in any one volume. Furthermore the only way to actually learn to sail is in a boat. However, I hope after you have finished reading this book, which has something in it for all types of beginners, you will feel that I have helped you in some measure to bring the wonderful sport of sailing a little closer to you.

GEORGE D. O'DAY

Boston, Mass.

SAIL
in a
DAY!

Sailfish racing on Cape Cod Sound. (Courtesy Howey Caufman)

Schooner or dinghy, five sails or one, the principles of sailing are the same. (Courtesy Dorothy Crossley)

1. An Invitation to Sail

How many times have you driven by a lake or river or ocean harbor on a hot summer day and noticed how inviting the sailboats looked?

As you stopped your car for a minute to watch the graceful craft weave in and around one another in a symphony of motion, haven't you thought how nice it would be if one of the boats pulled up close to you and someone shouted, "Say, how'd you like to go for a sail?"

Chances are it won't happen just that way, but with sailboats becoming increasingly popular each year, you're bound to get a call from a friend, neighbor or relative who has just bought a boat and wants you to go for a sail.

If you've never stepped foot in a sailboat before, there are a few things you should know and appreciate about sailing craft that will make your first sail more enjoyable than if you go aboard totally unaware of what to expect.

Your prospective host, the new boat owner (or maybe your first host afloat will be an "old salt"), will be interested to know if you have had any sailing experience. I can think of no other sport in which it is more vital to make it clear to the skipper that this will be your first experience at it. He's going to find out anyway the moment you are aboard, so you might as well square with him right from the beginning, while you're still on land. Of course, if you have been a guest on board before on another boat, or taken a few lessons,

by all means let this be known. Skippers can always use an extra pair of hands, preferably experienced. But don't overestimate your ability; it could get you into serious trouble.

The problem of what to wear is not a difficult one. Sports clothes, of course, with particular attention to the footwear. Rubber-soled shoes are an absolute must. This does not mean the 98-cent one-thong rubber sandals popular for beachwear. It does mean a sneaker-type of shoe with a definite tread like a herringbone bottom to grip the deck or floor.

For the ladies, something on the head is rather important. A wide-brimmed sun hat shades the eyes, but doesn't work too well in the wind, which is apt to carry it away, and the brim can get caught in the rigging with possible disastrous results to milady's hairdo. More appropriate would be a scarf that ties under the chin or a cap or narrow-brimmed straw, either one of which must fit very snugly or tie under the chin.

As far as yachting clothing is concerned, as a beginner you would do well to forget about a yachting cap until you are sure you want to be a yachtsman. (And even yachtsmen seldom wear them.) Dressed to "look the part" might prove embarrassing if you find yourself losing an oar, tripping over a line, or worse yet, falling into the water.

If your first sail is on a cool day, a windproof or waterproof jacket is the best bet, with a sweater or two underneath. Extra clothing can always be taken off, but if you don't bring along sufficient apparel to begin with, there's little chance of finding substitutes at sea.

You will, doubtless, want to take your sunglasses sailing with you, if it is a terrifically bright day. If they are expensive ones, make sure they fit you well or have a light line tied around the back of your head from stem to stern. Sneaking a look "over the side" might result in the contribution of your glasses to Davy Jones' locker.

Unless you are prone to seasickness you don't need any Dramamine if the sailboat on which you are going to have a ride is a small one. If, however, it is a craft large enough to have a cabin with bunks to sleep in, a toilet (head) and cooking space (a galley), you may be more comfortable having taken some in case the weather suddenly becomes unpleasant.

If you and your wife have been invited for the sail, don't appear with a lot of extra people. The sailboat may not be large enough to accommodate your mother-in-law and your neighbors. Unlike powerboats, a ride in a sailboat requires some moving around, particularly on the part of the skipper, and an overcrowded boat can't be maneuvered efficiently.

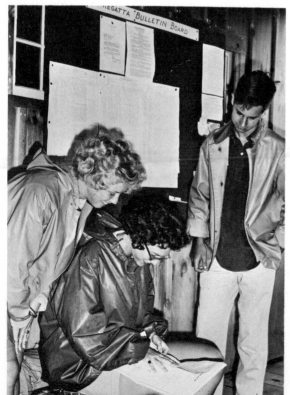

Leave your camera at home unless the boat on which you are sailing is a large one (20 feet or more), and then only if the skipper says OK. Keeping a camera dry on board a small sailboat is not an easy job, and spray will ruin it. In fact, never bring along unnecessary extras on this first trip. If it's a picnic, and you have volunteered to bring the lunch, pack it (duffle bag technique) in something similar to an airline plastic bag with a zipper closing. It takes up little space and keeps the lunch dry. Cold drinks in cans ride better in a sailboat than anything in a bottle. Bottles can get dislodged and roll around in the boat and break.

Will I get wet in a sailboat? This question is frequently asked by the uninitiated.

Everything depends on the size and design of the boat, the weather, the skipper and the courtesy of the other boats on the waterway. It is quite possible that you will have a completely dry sail, but you will do well to think about some dry spot (a weather-proof pocket) to put your watch or your wallet should the boat turn out to be the type that takes a little spray over the side.

Getting in and out of a small sailboat requires a little concentration. The temptation is to keep one foot on the dock and the other in the boat. This is a sure way to end up in the "drink." The trick is not to dilly-dally between boat and dock, simply step right into the boat, aiming for the most central point (amidships). If you enter the boat too close to its bow or too close to its stern, you can tip the craft over if it is small.

For this very first sailboat ride, it is better to stay on the dock and wait for instructions from your host before boarding. Don't be too concerned about making yourself useful. Those who try too eagerly to help only get in the skipper's way. After you have been

These youngsters are dressed to go sailing in their "foul weather" gear.
This waterproof apparel is available in a variety of styles for both men and women. (Courtesy Dorothy Crossley)

12

This group is sensibly dressed for sailing, particularly the child. (A life jacket is a must *for children.) Note the rubber-soled, tie-on type of shoe they are all wearing. Note also the height of the boom. The girl on the left will have to look sharp when coming about. (Courtesy Dorothy Crossley)*

advised exactly when and how to board the boat, sit where you are told to sit until further instructions. While you are thinking and waiting for things to happen, cast your eyes about to see what the inside of the boat looks like before you get under way and the sails are up. It will probably seem to you that the thrashing noises the sails make, flapping in the breeze, is not only annoying, but frightening. To the uninitiated, the flapping of sails is disturbing, but notice how quietly the sails perform once the boat is underway.

Now that you are about to leave the dock or the mooring, the first thing that may trouble you a little is the way the boat starts to tip (heel) and your first reaction may be one of unsteadiness with an urge to move to a "safer place." This tipping or heeling is all very normal for all types of sailboats,

although some skippers like to heel their boats more than others. You will soon discover this is all part of the fun and begin to enjoy it.

One thing to keep your eye on aboard a sailboat is the boom—the horizontal bar just above your head that seems to be almost as long as the boat. Many booms move back and forth over your head with ample clearance, but on some smaller boats they are just low enough so that you must duck when they start to swing. Don't ever stand up unless instructed to. Your skipper will tell you when he is going to change the position of the boat against the wind. This is called changing tack, and in so doing he will change the position of the boom.

He will probably yell, "Ready about, hard alee." This is the warning to watch out for the boom, particularly if you have also been asked by the skipper to move to the other side of the boat. The side highest out of the water, of course.

On some boats you may not be asked to move at all. However, on the others, by the time you have finished your afternoon sail you will feel as though the number of times you have changed your place and moved around on the boat will have provided you with the same amount of exercise as a game of tennis.

Once your sail is underway, and a small amount of water has accumulated in the boat, you may find it more comfortable to remove your shoes and put them in the sailbag or in some other dry place. But remember, bare feet are dangerous on a boat. Should you decide to scamper about the boat in your bare feet, bear in mind that the inside of the sailboat can be an obstacle course, which you

may find a little difficult to master at first. Also fiberglass is smoother than a skating rink. Such things as floorboards, cleats, bailing devices, oars, and so forth are a few of the things your bare feet will have to reckon with, to say nothing of the mass of rope and lines that make the deck or cockpit look like a plate of spaghetti. In short, leave your sneakers on.

On any boat, whether it be a powerboat or a sailboat on a race or a cruise, there can be only one boss, and that's the skipper. If you want to be invited more than once aboard someone's sailboat, even if you have already read a hundred volumes on how to sail, never at any point argue with the skipper. He is making every effort to make you comfortable on his boat, and he needs your full cooperation.

Through some change in the weather, he

Newcomers to sailing are frequently apprehensive about the way a sailboat tips, or "heels." Extreme heeling is usually done for the benefit of photographers, but a certain angle of heel is not only safe but efficient for all sailcraft. These two young sailors are Pamela O'Day, daughter of the author, and Trippie Mosbacher, son of the racing skipper. (Courtesy Howey Caufman)

A skipper and his guests relax before an afternoon of sailing. This craft is a Columbia Sabre. (Beckner Photo Service)

may need to enlist your help to handle the smaller of the two sails, called the jib. When he gives the instructions as to what to do with the small sail, it will be to your advantage to do exactly what he says when he says it and ask "why" later on when you're back on shore.

One of the things which you must watch out for in a sailboat (particularly a small one) is that never at any time do you sit or put your foot on a piece of rope called the "line" or "sheet." This you must constantly watch out for each time you move around in a sailboat. If the line needs to run out in a hurry because there is suddenly too much wind in the sail, it is not going to run at all if you are sitting on it, or if it is wrapped around your ankle or your arm.

In a small sailboat of the type where you may be asked to change your position each time the boat changes its "tack," you will find the routine very easy to get used to. Basically, there are three things to keep in mind when the skipper says, "Ready about, hard alee."

1. Remove yourself as quickly and gracefully as possible from where you are sitting to the opposite side of the boat (the higher side).

2. While you are doing this, be very careful that you do not get hit with the boom.

3. While you are making this maneuver and after having made it, be certain that you have not become entangled in any of the ropes or coiled or uncoiled line in the boat.

There are a few things to remember if you

15

are invited aboard a yacht as a guest for a weekend.

Bear in mind that space aboard any kind of boat is limited even if it's a 40-footer. You are not the only guest to be invited—the bigger the boat the more people there may be on it! Better inquire of the skipper as to what clothes to bring. The ladies need not pack a dress and high-heeled shoes if there are no plans to go ashore to a yacht club or expensive restaurant for dining, etc. Also, if the host keeps an extra supply of foul weather clothes aboard you won't need to buy, borrow, or bring any. But bring plenty of bathing suits; they don't dry well aboard, and you may be living in a bathing suit.

You would be wise to bring your own toothpaste, soap, towel and Kleenex. The ladies may find it hard to manage their hairdos aboard and will want to bring a good supply of scarves, or something that anchors well on the head.

Bear in mind when you board your host's yacht, that this is his pride and joy and treat it as such. Make sure that your greasy suntan lotion doesn't get on the expensive teak or mahogany trim on the boat. If it does, it could be your last boat ride. Better to select a non-greasy lotion.

Keep your cigarette ashes away from sails —nylon or dacron burns readily. Better to inquire first before you light a cigarette if it is all right to do so.

Watch out that you don't sit on cushions and upholstery in a dripping bathing suit. It takes a long time for these mattresses and cushions to dry out. Stay topside or change quickly into a dry suit.

If you are a woman with an urge to help out in the kitchen or galley, you will discover that your skipper will probably prefer to manage everything himself. He's used to the stove and its peculiarities and the other equipment. If he needs help he'll ask you and tell you just what to do.

Refrain from asking questions such as: "Why are we turning around?" "What is that rope doing there?" The silent pleasant guest, if new to sailing, is usually the most popular one aboard.

Last, but not least, read and heed the directions in the "head" for using the marine toilet. And don't be shy; if you run into a complication, don't keep it to yourself. You're not on a train, you're on a boat, and marine toilets can create a serious problem if they are not functioning properly.

Once you have been aboard a friend's boat you will soon observe the type of guests who get invited more than once and have a front seat ticket as opposed to those who don't, and no one will have to tell you the reasons why.

This guest makes himself useful while underway. Modern yachts are so designed that even a 40-footer like this can be sailed with efficiency by one or two persons. (Beckner Photo Service)

The well-known racing sailboat, the Olympic 5.5 meter, being skippered by the author. Note the small cockpit. Here, crewing is raised to the level of art.

2. Learning to Sail Without a Boat

Before you have a boat of your own or have occasion to skipper a boat, there is much you can do to prepare to become a skipper by watching what others do. You will be way ahead of the game if you simply take a diagram of a sailboat and memorize the parts. When you are a guest on board someone's sailboat or crewing for someone, and he tells you to trim the jib you will know what it is and where it is. This is just common sense. Although some people have learned to sail without paying much attention to the sailing vernacular, if you are dependent on someone else teaching you to sail, you will make yourself more valuable to him by boning up on some of the terminology. You can find the terminology used in this book in the glossary. We have illustrated the glossary to make it easier for you to hitch a name to a part. The three or four basic knots that you really ought to learn as a beginner in sailing can be found in this book and in almost any book on boating. A thorough knowledge of a few knots which can be practiced at home easily can make you valuable on a sailboat if you are a beginner, and particularly valuable as crew.

Good crewing is an art in itself. Although your indoctrination as a guest on board a sailboat 35 feet long is perhaps a lot more comfortable than being indoctrinated to sailing on a 16-footer, if you want to learn to sail with opportunity to crew, the 16-footer is going to make it a lot easier for you to get to learn the sport. Sensitivity is needed by each crew member, as well as an ability to move about the boat smoothly and gracefully. A gentle adjustment of a line on a small sailboat makes for far more efficient sailing than a jerky yank on the same line.

When you are crewing on a small boat you are no longer actually a guest, particularly if you are crewing during a race. It will not be possible for you to relax because your responsibility will be to watch the jib (the smaller sail), and to be continually responding with your weight to the changes in the wind. A boat well crewed by a pair who have sailed a great deal together is a symphony of harmony and a balanced blending of skills.

On some boats as part of your training as crew you will be expected not only to handle the jib and make other adjustments on board the boat, such as raising and lowering the sails, but you will have to be concerned with the intricate, sometimes difficult, art of setting the spinnaker (the big parachute-like sail that billows out in front of the sailboat when it is going downwind).

When you do locate someone who has offered to let you crew for them in exchange for sailing lessons, you will discover that some people have a Dr. Jekyll and Mr. Hyde personality when they are skippers of a boat. When you talk with them and know them on shore they appear to be a good-natured, soft-voiced, even-tempered personality. However, once out on the water at the helm of a sailboat, they can somehow suddenly turn into monsters shrieking out orders to the crew with the gentleness of a master sergeant in the Army. If you are the kind that doesn't mind being shouted at while you are learning to sail, it might be worth your while to put up with the noise. However, if you are sensitive, you may find yourself looking for a type of skipper who can teach you how to sail without raising his or her voice much above a whisper. There are a few like this, but don't expect them to bother with a "please" or "thank you" during a race. There just isn't time even with the most even-tempered of skippers.

A fleet of racer-cruisers sailing to windward during a race off Seal Beach, Calif. Crewing under these conditions is a bit more relaxed, but still in earnest. (Beckner Photo Service)

3. Illustrated Glossary

Illustrations by Mary S. Shakespeare

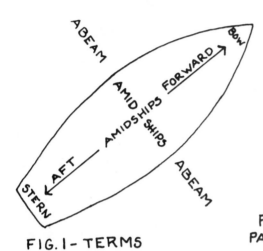

FIG. 1 – TERMS

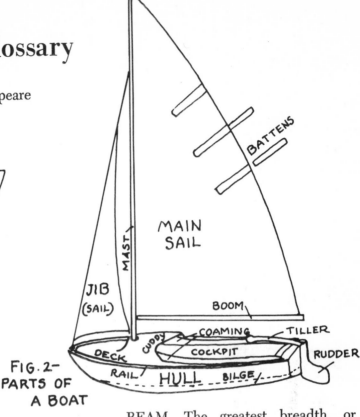

FIG. 2 –
PARTS OF
A BOAT

ABAFT. Toward the stern.

ABEAM. The direction at right angles to the line of the keel.

AFT. At, toward, or near the stern.

AMIDSHIPS. The part of a vessel midway from bow to stern, or inboard from her sides.

BACKSTAYS. Ropes or wires slanting sharply aft from the mast for the purpose of supporting this spar. Stays requiring adjustment with each change of tack are known as *running backstays* (runners), while one leading directly to the stern is termed a *permanent backstay*.

BALLAST. Iron or lead placed low inside a boat to increase stability by lowering the center of gravity. Lead and iron keels are termed outside ballast to distinguish from inside ballast.

BATTENS. Thin wooden or plastic strips used to hold the leech of a sail and prevent curling. *Batten pockets* hold the battens in sails.

BLOCKS

BIGHT

BEAM. The greatest breadth, or width, of a vessel.

BEAT. A course of action by which a boat sails to windward. *Beating* is sailing to windward by a series of tacks, although the phrase *beating to leeward* is used when a boat sails down the wind on a series of jibes.

BEND. To make a sail fast to a spar or stay by means of groove or track, knots, or snaphooks. To secure with a bend.

BIGHT. A curve in a rope before it becomes a loop. However, the expressions "caught in" or "by a bight" are used when it closes around a limb or object.

BILGE. The turn of the hull below the waterline; also that part inside the hull where bilge water collects above or near keel.

BLOCK. A nautical form of pulley with one or more rollers (sheaves).

BOOM. A spar at the foot of a fore-and-aft sail; also a pole used to

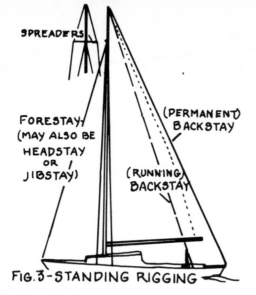

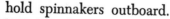

FIG. 3 - STANDING RIGGING

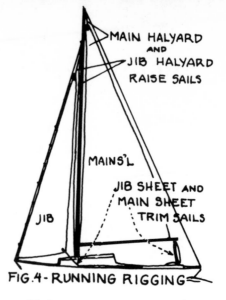

FIG. 4 - RUNNING RIGGING

hold spinnakers outboard.

BOW. The forward part of a vessel. Also, curve of the stem.

BROACH. To swing sharply toward wind when sailing free due to heavy seas, poor steering, etc.

BURDENED VESSEL. A craft required to keep clear of vessel holding the right of way.

CENTERBOARD. A movable, pivoted device of wood, plastic, or metal, used in place of a keel to give stability, permit sailing in shallower waters than keel craft, and prevent sliding away from wind (leeway). When raised, it is housed in a centerboard trunk. The daggerboard, a sliding form of centerboard which has no pivot, may only be lowered or lifted vertically.

CHAIN PLATES. Metal plates bolted to the side of a boat to which stays are attached to support rigging.

CHARTS. Nautical maps, giving aids to navigation, water depths, shoals, currents, landmarks, etc.

CHOCK. A metal casting, usually at the bow, through which mooring and securing lines or ropes are led.

CLEAT. A piece of wood or metal with two horns around which ropes are made fast.

CLEW. The lower aft corner of a fore-and-aft or triangular sail.

CHAIN PLATE

CRINGLE

CHOCK

CLEAT

CLOSE-HAULED. Sailing as close to the wind as possible, with sails trimmed for beating to windward.

CLOSE-WINDED. A craft capable of sailing very close to the wind.

COAMING. A raised protection around the cockpit of a small boat.

COCKPIT. The undecked portion of a small boat where the helmsman steers and crew sits. It may be a well, usually watertight and sometimes self-bailing, aft of the cuddy or cabinhouse on a keel boat. All other cockpits are called open.

CRINGLE. A metal or rope eye worked into a clew, tack, or head of a sail for securing purposes.

CUDDY. A decked shelter, less formal than a cabin, usually aft of the mast.

DEADWOOD. The solid timbers between keel and hull proper.

DOWNHAUL. A rope or tackle by which a sail is pulled downward, usually to improve its shape.

DRAFT. The depth of water needed to float a boat.

DRY SAILING. When boats are stored ashore on trailers or cradles between each use, or transported overland from port to port to race or cruise.

EASE. To relieve pressure on sail or helm—to pay out a sheet, to luff, etc.

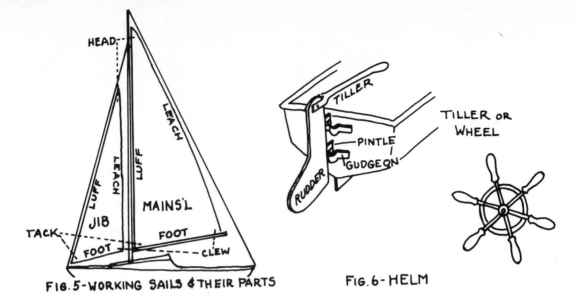

FIG. 5—WORKING SAILS & THEIR PARTS

FIG. 6—HELM

FAIRLEAD. An eye or fitting which changes the direction of a sheet or rope led through it. Many boats have adjustable fairleads.

FALL. The hauling part of a rope; also the standing part.

FETCH. When a craft sailing to windward can make its objective without another tack.

FIN. A thin projection from the underbody for steadying and stability purpose. In sailboats, usually a narrow, deep keel—often of metal —with bulbous section at bottom.

FLY. Usually a masthead pennant, pointer, or windsock to assist skipper in determining *apparent wind* direction as related to boat, which may not be exactly the same as *true wind* direction. Bits of yarn tied to rigging for same purpose.

FOOT. Lower edge of a sail. *Forefoot* is where stem joins keel.

FORE-AND-AFT. The rig used on most small sailboats—technically in line with the keel.

FOREMAST. The forward mast of a schooner (see diagram of rigs).

FRAMES. The ribs to which planking is attached, with sometimes a fine distinction made between ribs and heavier, less numerous frames interspersed between series of ribs.

FREE. Sailing with the wind any-

FAIRLEADS

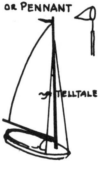

FLY --WINDSOCK OR PENNANT

TELLTALE

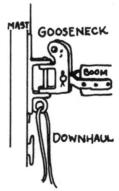

MAST GOOSENECK

BOOM

DOWNHAUL

where from abeam to due aft. Also means to cast off, untangle, permit to run easily.

FREEBOARD. Vertical distance from waterline to deck.

GAFF. Spar hoisted on aft side of mast to support head of a sail, hence *gaff-rigged*.

GARBOARD (strake). Plank nearest to keel.

GENOA. A large, overlapping jib.

GOOSENECK. A metal fitting, normally a universal joint, securing boom to mast.

GUDGEON. An eye fitting to hold *pintles* of a rudder.

GUY. A rope or wire used to steady or support.

HALYARD (also HALLIARD or HALIARD). From Haulyard. Rope or wire used to hoist sails.

HARD-A-LEE. Final command used in tacking a boat, i.e. coming about.

HEAD. Upper corner of sail. Also a boat's toilet. *Headboard* is a wooden, plastic, or metal fitting at head of sail.

HEADSTAY. Usually the forward stay supporting a mast, sometimes called *forestay*, but some boats have both.

HEAD-TO-WIND. With bow headed into wind and sails shaking.

23

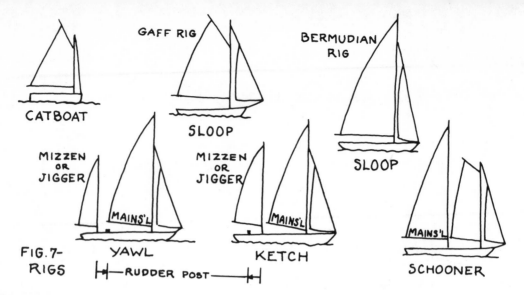

GAFF RIG — CATBOAT — SLOOP — BERMUDIAN RIG — SLOOP

MIZZEN OR JIGGER — MAINS'L — FIG. 7- RIGS — YAWL — RUDDER POST

MIZZEN OR JIGGER — MAINS'L — KETCH

MAINS'L — SCHOONER

HEADWAY. Forward motion of a boat.

HEAVE. To throw, but also to haul in or upon. *Heave-to*, lying with a boat's bow held head-to-wind.

HEEL. The tilt, tip, list, heeling, or laying-over of a boat, usually due to wind.

HELM. The tiller or wheel used to steer a boat. With tillers, to put *helm down* turns toward wind as in tacking, *helm up* away from as in jibing. *Helmsman*, one who steers.

HIKE. To climb or to lean out to windward to counteract excessive heeling.

HULL. The main body of a boat as distinct from spars, sails, and gear.

IN STAYS or IN IRONS. When head-to-wind while tacking. When a craft remains in stays unduly long with no way she is *In Irons*.

JIB. A triangular sail set forward of foremast on schooner. The inner of two jibs is a *forestaysail*.

JIBE or GYBE. To change tacks by turning away from the wind with the boom shifting from one side to the other. See also *Beating*.

JIB-HEAD or JIB-HEADED. A tall rig with triangular mainsail, often miscalled Marconi. *Bermudian rig* is perfectly correct.

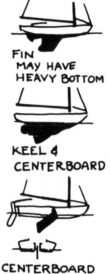

FIN MAY HAVE HEAVY BOTTOM

KEEL & CENTERBOARD

CENTERBOARD

JUMPER STRUT

SPREADER

JIBSTAY. The forward stay on which jib is hoisted.

JIGGER. The shorter, aft mast of a yawl or ketch.

JUMPER STRUT. A single or forked strut for added support placed aloft on forward side of a mast.

KEEL. The lowest permanent part of the hull, hence the backbone of a boat. In keel yachts it extends deep below the rest of the hull. In centerboard boats, it is the central timber through which the board lowers. See *Fin*.

KNEE. A timber with two arms connecting frames and beams to give added strength.

KNOT. A measure of speed, one nautical mile per hour. The tying or securing of a rope to objects or other rope, including the tying of loops in a rope.

LAY. Of a rope, the direction of the twist of yarns, or other fiber parts in the making of *strands, ropes,* and *cables*. To *lay,* same as to *Fetch*.

LAZARETTE. A small enclosed space under the deck near stern.

LEACH. The aft edge of a fore-and-aft or triangular sail.

LEE or LEEWARD. Away from the direction of the wind, hence *lee* side, and to *leeward*. *Lee shore,* against which the wind is blowing.

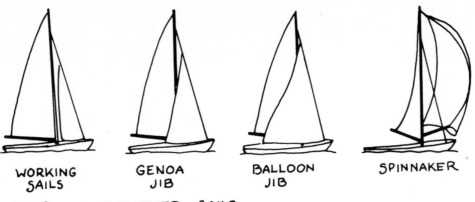

WORKING SAILS   GENOA JIB   BALLOON JIB   SPINNAKER

FIG. 8 - LIGHTWEATHER SAILS

Lee or *leeward helm,* an unbalanced condition which turns the boat's bow away from the wind. *Lee bow,* an object off the bow to leeward or a force against the bow from leeward, *lee bow tide. In the lee,* behind the boat, land, or object to windward. *By the lee,* running to leeward with the wind and boom on the same side.

LIGHT SAILS. Spinnakers and other sails of light materials used to increase boat's speed off the wind.

LINES. General term for light ropes, also used for any running rigging. Drawings showing the shapes of hulls.

LUFF. The forward edge of a fore-and-aft sail. Also the shaking of a sail when a boat points too high for her trim. The spilling of wind from a sail. To turn toward the wind, the first action in tacking, or for tactical and sheet-trimming purposes.

MAINMAST. The principal mast of a sloop, catboat, yawl, or ketch; the taller aft mast of a two-masted schooner.

MAINSAIL. The *triangular,* fore-and-aft sail set on the aft side of a mainmast.

MAINSHEET. The rope by which a boom or sail is pulled in or slacked

MOORING BUOYS

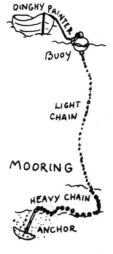

DINGHY PAINTER

BUOY

LIGHT CHAIN

MOORING

HEAVY CHAIN

ANCHOR

off, usually through a system of blocks.

MARCONI. A tall mast used with the jib-headed or Bermudian rig. *Not a rig.*

MAST. A vertical spar supporting sails and rigging. See *Main, Fore,* and *Mizzen* masts.

MIZZEN. The small aft mast on a yawl or ketch. See also *Jigger.*

MOORING. The relatively permanent anchor or weight to which a yacht rides by means of chain, rope, and pennant, when not sailing. *To moor* is to pick up a *mooring buoy* and secure to a mooring.

OFFSHORE. Away from, or a wind blowing off, the shore.

OFF THE WIND. Sailing on any course except to windward.

ON THE WIND. Close hauled.

OUTBOARD. Beyond a boat's side or hull.

OUTHAUL. A line used to secure the *clew* of a sail.

OVERSTAND. To go beyond an objective, usually unintentionally.

PAINTER. A short piece of rope securing the bow of a boat to a landing or other object.

PARACHUTE. A spinnaker cut so as to resemble a parachute.

PART. To break. Also, the hauling, standing, or running part of a rope.

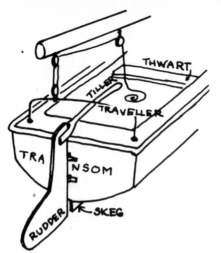

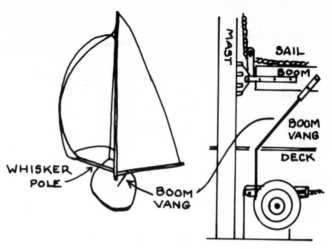

FIG. 9 - MORE PARTS OF A BOAT   **FIG 10- BOOM VANG**

PAY OFF, PAY OUT. A boat *pays off* when her bow turns away from the wind. *Pay out* is to slacken.

PENNANT. A small, narrow flag. A wire or rope by which a mooring is attached to the boat.

PINCH. To sail a boat so close to the wind that her sails shake or her progress slows.

PINTLE. A metal, pin-like fitting allowing a rudder to swing when inserted in the *gudgeon*.

POINT, POINTING. To head high, rather close to the wind.

PORT. The left side of a boat when looking forward. *Port Tack*, when the wind blows over the port side.

PRIVILEGED VESSEL. A vessel holding the right of way, required to hold her course.

QUARTER. The part of a boat's side aft of *abeam* and forward of the *stern*.

RAIL. The outer edge of the deck.

RAKE. The inclination of a mast from the vertical.

RAP FULL. With all sails drawing full, just a little off the wind.

REACH, REACHING. All sailing courses between close-hauled and running. *Close reach*, sailing nearly close-hauled with sheets just *eased*. *Beam reach*, sailing with the wind *abeam*. *Broad reach*, sailing with

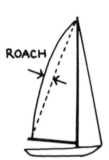

ROACH

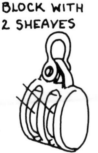

BLOCK WITH
2 SHEAVES

the wind *abaft the beam* and with sails well out on the *quarter*.

READY ABOUT. Preparatory order when tacking.

REEVE. To pass rope, sheet, or halyard through block, fairlead, etc.

RIB. See *Frame*.

RIDE. To lie at anchor. *Hove-to* in a storm (ride out).

RIG. The character of a boat's mast and sail arrangement. *Jib-head* rig, *gaff* rig, *cat* rig, etc.

RIGGING. The wires and ropes of a boat. *Running rigging* sets or trims sails. (Standing rigging is permanently secured rigging.)

ROACH. The outward curve of the *leach* of a sail.

RODE. Anchor line of a small boat.

RUN, RUNNING. To sail almost directly before the wind. The aft underwater part of a boat's hull is called *run*.

SEAWAY. Place where rough or moderate seas are running. A well traveled waterway.

SECURE. To make fast.

SET. The shape of a sail. The direction of tide. The pushing of a boat to *leeward* of its course. *Set up*, or *taut*, to take in, take up, usually in order to relieve strain, or improve shape of a sail.

SHACKLE. A U-shaped metal fitting with a pin or screw across the open end used to join halyards and ropes to sails or other objects.

SHEAVE. The wheel in a block.

SHEER. The curve of the deck between bow and stern. *Sheer off*, to bear away. *Sheer strake*, topmost plank on the side of a boat.

SHROUDS. Wires or ropes supporting mast. Also, supporting bowsprits and outriggers.

SKEG. An extension or protrusion of the keel aft, usually to aid steering or support an outboard rudder.

SKIPPER. Person in command. In sailing, skipper is often used interchangeably with *helmsman* on small boats.

SLIP. To cast off. Also, a mooring area between small piers or floating booms.

SPAR. General term for masts, booms, gaffs, etc.

SPINNAKER. A light sail used when running and reaching, and held out from the mast by a *spinnaker pole* or *boom*.

SPREADER. A horizontal strut to which shrouds or stays are attached, to support the mast and spread rigging.

STARBOARD. The right side of a boat when looking forward. A boat sails on *starboard tack* when the wind blows over starboard side.

STAYS. Ropes and wires supporting masts. *Shrouds* are special stays, usually on each side of mast. See also *Backstay, Forestay, Jibstay, Headstay*.

STEM. The foremost timber at the bow of a boat. Stems may be plastic or metal.

STERN. The aft extremity of a boat.

STRAKE. Any plank on the side or bottom of a hull. See *Garboard* and *Sheer* strakes.

JIFFY SHACKLE

SNAP SHACKLE

TACK. The forward lower corner of a fore-and-aft or triangular sail. A boat when under way sails on a *tack*, either starboard or port. For example, *starboard tack* when the wind blows over her starboard side. A boat *tacks* when she changes from *starboard* to *port* tack or vice versa by turning toward the wind. She is then said to have made a *tack*.

TAUT. Stretched tight, snug.

TENDER. A sailboat lacking sufficient stability, opposite of stiff. Also a dinghy-type craft which may be rowed or sailed.

THWARTS. Seats that go across the cockpit of a small boat, *thwartship*.

TILLER. A wooden bar or rod used to steer small boats by fitting to the top of the rudder or rudder-post. Called "stick" at times. Tiller extensions are known also as *hiking sticks*.

TOPSIDES. Usually the sides of the boat lying between waterline and rail. In a broad sense, any above-water part of the hull.

TRANSOM. Usually applied to mean a broad stern that is a straight or almost vertical line from the deck to the water. It may be planked, a single board, or molded. Loosely, transom is sometimes used almost interchangeably with stern. A long stern tapering from the waterline to the sternboard is called a *counter* or yacht stern.

TRAVELLER. Metal rod on which sheet blocks slide athwartships for trimming purposes. Rope or wire travellers are technically *bridles*.

TRIM. To set sails correctly in relation to the wind by means of sheets. The fore-and-aft balance of a boat. Also used in relation to *thwartship* balance, i.e., with *heeling* and *hiking*.

TUNING. The delicate adjustment of a boat's rigging, sails, and hull to the proper balance which assures the best sailing performance.

TURNBUCKLE. A threaded link which pulls two eyes together for setting up standing rigging.

VANG. A wire or a rope used to steady a spar—most common usage, *boom vang*.

VEER. A shift of the wind in a clockwise direction, or toward the stern. The wind may *haul* aft or clockwise, however. When the wind shifts counterclockwise, it *backs*.

WAKE. The foamy disturbed water left astern by a moving boat.

WATERLINE. Where a boat floats in the water when properly trimmed, the division line between underbody and topsides. Often a distinctive painted stripe called the *boot-topping* or *top*.

WAY. Movement through the water. A boat's forward way is *headway*; backward, *sternway*; and any movement, *underway*, especially immediately after leaving a mooring or landing.

WEATHER. A synonym for *windward*.

WELL FOUND. A well-equipped boat with all gear in good condition.

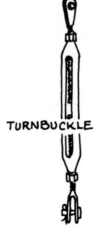

TURNBUCKLE

WINCH

WING, & WING

WHISKER-POLE. A light pole or stick used to pole out a jib to *windward* to permit sailing *wing-and-wing* on a run, when a spinnaker is not set.

WINCH. A small drum-shaped mechanical device, similar to a windlass, to increase hauling power on sheets and halyards.

WINDWARD. Toward the wind, hence the *weather* side of a boat, and *to windward*. *Windward* and *weather* are almost interchangeable in speaking of *windward shore*, *weather bow*, and *windward helm*. A *weather helm* is one which tends to turn the boat's bow toward the wind, a desirable feature if not too strong. See *Lee* and *Leeward*.

WING-AND-WING. When jib and mainsail, or any two working sails of a boat are trimmed from the opposite sides.

WORKING SAILS. The ordinary fore-and-aft sails, such as jib and mainsail, exclusive of light sails or storm sails.

YACHT. Any craft, regardless of size, used for pleasure, from a rowboat to Her Majesty Queen Elizabeth's *Britannia*.

YAW. The side-to-side swinging of a boat due to steering badly in a *seaway*.

4. A Few Knots and a Word About Rigging

Webster defines a "line" in many different ways, but for our purposes—a discussion of the use of lines—we'll assume a line to be a rope used in mooring, anchoring, or rigging. Actually, nothing betrays the inexperienced sailor more quickly than the condition of his lines. This stems from the old days of the sailing vessel when a ship's lines were among its most important gear. Lines are still extremely important, and keeping them shipshape is just as vital in a small sailing rig as it was to the sailors of ocean-going clippers.

To fasten lines we must use knots, and it behooves the sailboat skipper to have a rudimentary knowledge of the more common knots in order to make his lines fast properly to a pier or wharf and to fasten his mooring and other pieces of equipment that must be well secured.

Always be sure that your mooring lines are secured to strong bitts or cleats. So that they will be ready for instant use, all lines, including halyard, should be coiled. To coil a line for easy running, lay it down from right to left in a circle, beginning with the inboard end and laying each turn on or slightly inside the previous one so that they will feed off easily without fouling. Lash them that way with one or two pieces of cord tied for quick release. Or if the rope is to be moved about or hung up, pick up the coiled rope on your forearm, leaving about five or six feet of line between it and the anchor or the bitt. Turn your arm to wrap the line twice around the entire coil. Pull a line of the remaining line through the coil above the wrap, bring it back and down over the upper coil. If unlashed carefully, it will remain free-running for instant use.

You don't make a line fast to a cleat simply by winding it around as on a spool, but by crisscrossing over the top of the cleat to the opposite side after every turn. This makes for greater security, so learn this simple operation now.

Another helpful practice is either to back-splice or "whip" the ends. Back-splicing may be learned from any old salt (who might even do it for you). To whip the ends, simply wrap them with waxed hemp or with plastic tape so that the ends can't fray. If your rope is nylon or orlon, fraying can be prevented by singeing the end of the rope. All of these methods protect the ends of the line from fraying and forming what is known as "cow-tails."

One of the most useful knots for a sailor is the clove hitch, which is used extensively for temporary moorings. It's easily tied and has the added advantage of holding tighter the harder it's pulled. It also resists slipping down a post or piling and, most important, is easy to untie.

In making fast to a bollard, stanchion, or timber, use the clove hitch. Or you can make one turn around the object and then a clove hitch or two half hitches on the standing (or holding) part of the line. A half hitch is also useful in making fast to a cleat. Simply pass

KNOWING HOW HALYARDS AND OTHER LINES ARE MADE FAST TO SMALL CLEATS IS A MUST.

CLEAT HITCH

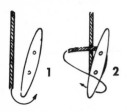

1 & 2 — MAKE A TURN AROUND BASE OF CLEAT;

3 — A TURN AROUND LOWER HORN;

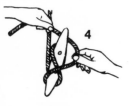

4 — A TURN UNDER UPPER HORN WITH A BIGHT HELD OPEN.

5 — TUCK A LOOP OF WORKING END UNDER BIGHT.

6 — PULL LOOP DOWNWARD, MAKING ALL TIGHT. TO RELEASE, PULL LOOSE END AND UNWIND.

THE **BOWLINE** MAKES A NON-SLIPPING LOOP, EASY TO UNTIE, MOST USEFUL ON SEA AND LAND. NOTE THAT THE PRIME FEATURE IS AN EYE WITH AN END COMING UP THROUGH.

STANDING PART (TO BOAT) GRIP HERE (SEE 2) — ON TOP — EYE — WORKING END

LEAVE LOOSE — PULL — PULL

A — B

1. MAKE AN EYE AS ABOVE

2. BRING WORKING END UP THRU EYE.

3. CARRY END AROUND THE STANDING PART AND DOWN THRU EYE BESIDE ITSELF.

4. FINISH AS ABOVE, LEAVING LOOP LOOSE FOR EASY UNTYING.

A. TIED THRU RING. B. TIED AROUND, OR DROPPED OVER, A POST.

THE **FIGURE EIGHT** KNOT IS A "STOPPER" TO PREVENT DEVELOPMENTS SUCH AS THIS:

GOING!

GOING!!

GONE!!!

HERE'S HOW:

1

2

3

4

1. REMEMBER THE FIGURE EIGHT.

2 & 3. WEAVE THE LOOPS WITH END GOING ALTER-NATELY UNDER AND OVER.

4. PULL TIGHT.

WARNING!

NEVER TIE THIS FOR A FIGURE EIGHT. IT CAN'T BE UNTIED!

THE **SQUARE** OR **REEF** KNOT TIES TOGETHER TWO LINES OF THE SAME DIAMETER ONLY. (LINES OF DIFFERENT SIZES MAY BE JOINED BY TWO BOWLINES LINKED TOGETHER.)

1. CROSS ENDS

2. WEAVE ENDS TOGETHER AS ABOVE.

3. AGAIN CROSS ENDS. NOTE HOW.

4. WEAVE ENDS TOGETHER. PULL TIGHT.

FOR REEFING OR FURLING SQUARE KNOT WITH AN END LOOPED UNDER CAN BE QUICKLY UNTIED.

A **CLOVE HITCH** (TWO HALF HITCHES) AROUND A POST, SPAR, SIDESTAY IS VERY USEFUL.

SHAPED TOGETHER AND PULLED TIGHT.

TWO TURNS AND TWO HALF HITCHES

THIS FORMATION CAN ALSO BE MADE IN ANY PART OF A LINE AND DROPPED OVER A POST.

A GOOD TIE-UP

your line around the neck of the cleat, and then take a half hitch over one of the projections. If the half hitch that completes the fastening is taken with the free end of the line, the line can be cast off without taking up the slack on what is known as the standing part.

When a secure noose is needed for tying up to a post or piling, the bowline is a solid knot to use. Alternate tension and slack won't loosen this knot, which can also be used to fasten a line to an anchor and for various rigging applications. It is also the easiest of all sailing knots to untie, but one should be sure to keep his fingers out of the bight.

The square or reef knot, which everyone learned to tie as a kid, is used to tie lines together or for any other use where a solid, nonslip fastening is desired. It has many uses in boating.

One of the first steps toward becoming a sailor is to know how to rig a boat and this requires a familiarity with your boat's basic parts. Although all modern sailboats are different, to some degree, in hull structure and detail, the general working parts and sail plan are essentially the same.

Basic Parts—The forward part of any boat is called the *bow;* the rear is the *stern*. When one moves toward the stern, one moves *aft*. Looking forward toward the bow, the left-hand side is the *port* and the right-hand side is the *starboard*. (In giving steering directions, the U.S. Navy now uses left and right for port and starboard, though most amateur sailors still prefer the traditional usage, when they can remember it.) The glossary in Chapter 3 gives the names and illustrates other parts of the hull that you should be familiar with.

Construction—The hull construction material of a sailboat is an all-important consideration. While wood was the most popular material since the dawn of history, the majority of the boats manufactured for sailboat living today are of fiberglass, molded in layers of polyester plastic resin. The plastic, reinforced with fiberglass, is probably the strongest and most durable of all materials used in small-boat construction. The material is also immune to sea worms, termites, fungi, and bacteria; it doesn't rot, and water absorption is low.

While maintenance costs are greatly reduced with plastic hulls, it should be pointed out that the material isn't completely indestructible. Because of the great impact strength, the material won't dent or take an out-of-shape set—there are no internal stresses. Fiberglass will often deflect an impact and return to its original shape; if it does puncture or break, it can be repaired easily. Although plastic hulls don't require paint for preservation, they do need it for anti-fouling when used in salt-water and certain fresh-water areas. Also, the topsides of a fiberglass plastic boat may need paint for color, because the molded-in color will gradually fade with exposure to sunlight.

Since fiberglass hulls don't have the buoyancy of wood, flotation gear (a compartment containing buoyant material) is provided in most sailboats presently marketed. At the present time, the normal life of a fiberglass boat is still to be determined. The first hulls were constructed during the latter part of World War II, and as yet no serious deterioration has been detected. Laboratory tests, simulating actual use conditions, have shown these hulls to last at least thirty years with little or no indication of strength loss or deterioration of materials.

Shapes—Sailboat hulls are divided into two definite shapes: *centerboard* and *keel*. The main function of both is to furnish lateral resistance to keep the boat from sliding sideways through the water. There the resemblance ends.

The *centerboard* hull is shallow and has a wood, metal or fiberglass plate which moves up and down through a box on the centerline of the hull. Standard centerboards, the most commonly used type, are fitted with pins at their forward lower corners. At the after upper corner of each there's a line or chain arranged to control the depth of the centerboard.

Another style of centerboard that is often

found in small boats is the dagger type. This type requires a trunk and slot, but it isn't hinged; it is bodily lowered or raised. In fact, it can be entirely lifted out when the boat isn't being sailed. Adjustments are provided so that the depth of the centerboard below the bottom can be controlled, and often the slot and trunk are somewhat longer than the centerboard is wide so that the centerboard can be shifted forward or aft to provide perfect balance in relation to the center of sail pressure.

When sailing in shoal water or before the wind, and when at anchor, the centerboard is raised up into the trunk so that little, if any, of it projects below the bottom of the sailboat. However, most boats won't sail well when the centerboard is up except dead before the wind or on a broad reach.

For stability, this type of a boat relies on its wide beam and the weight of the crew. A centerboard craft can be capsized, but this is counteracted by the knowledge that it won't sink if buoyancy is built in. Furthermore, it is relatively inexpensive to build and maintain, and its light weight and fairly flat bottom make it easy to trailer. The draft of a centerboard sailboat can be as little as 3 inches. Most small sailing craft in the United States are of the centerboard type.

The *keel* in a small sailboat is built as an integral part of the hull and has a ballast weight attached to its bottom. If you have a choice between a sailboat with a keel and one with a centerboard, you should remember that each is a good craft if used under the circumstances for which it was designed.

In an area where the water is uniformly deep, the keel boat is generally preferable. If the water is shallow, the centerboard type is the best craft. The latter is also the better if speed is desired. Suppose two boats are built to the same lines and equipped with the same sail plan. On one, a centerboard is aboard; in the other a keel is installed. The craft with the centerboard will be the faster on all points of sailing except to windward, where the greater underwater area of the keel boat will allow it to point higher into the wind and make less leeway. Before the wind, the board on a centerboard boat can be raised, thus reducing the wetted surface. When coming about, the centerboard craft will be somewhat quicker because it has less area of lateral plane and because what area it does have is well centered. In centerboard boats the centerboard must be adjusted for the different points of sailing. This, of course, isn't necessary with a fixed keel.

The Rig—Within the scope of this book there are two basic rigs, or sail plans: the *cat* and the *sloop*.

The former, usually called a *catboat rig*, has a single mast, forward in the craft, and carries a single sail called the *mainsail* (mains'l). This type of rig in small boats is the simplest and easiest to learn with. However, unless it is exceptionally well designed, this rig won't sail very close into the wind, and coming about (going from one tack to the other) is sometimes difficult. Most of the familiar small sailing dinghies (under 10 feet) are cat-rigged.

The *sloop* rig has a single mast, but in addition to the mainsail it carries a jib or headsail forward of the mast. The sloop gives better control than the catboat because the sail area is broken up into two sails, which makes handling easier. For this reason, the sloop rig is recommended for all boats over 10 feet.

The basic rigging of a sailboat can be divided into three major categories: spar, standing rigging, and running rigging. The general term *spar* is given to the mast and boom.

Standing rigging consists of those lines, or *stays*, that are permanently fixed and that serve simply as supports for the mast. Those at the side of the mast are referred to as *sidestays* or *shrouds*. If your boat has a jib, a *forestay* or *jibstay* runs from the top, or near top, of the mast to the bow, and serves as a runner to which the jib is fastened by snap hooks and on which it is raised and lowered.

Running rigging consists of *halyards*, or ropes, used to hoist the sails and *sheets*, or ropes used to trim the sails to their position in

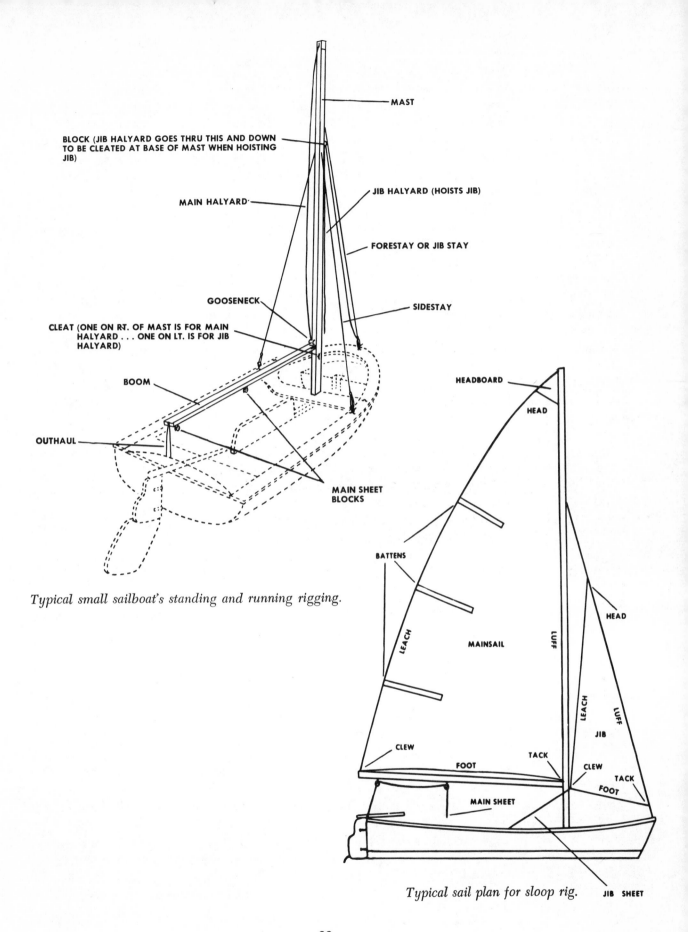

MAST

BLOCK (JIB HALYARD GOES THRU THIS AND DOWN TO BE CLEATED AT BASE OF MAST WHEN HOISTING JIB)

JIB HALYARD (HOISTS JIB)

MAIN HALYARD

FORESTAY OR JIB STAY

GOOSENECK

SIDESTAY

CLEAT (ONE ON RT. OF MAST IS FOR MAIN HALYARD . . . ONE ON LT. IS FOR JIB HALYARD)

BOOM

OUTHAUL

MAIN SHEET BLOCKS

Typical small sailboat's standing and running rigging.

HEADBOARD

HEAD

BATTENS

HEAD

LEACH

MAINSAIL

LUFF

LEACH

LUFF

JIB

CLEW

FOOT

TACK

CLEW

TACK

FOOT

MAIN SHEET

JIB SHEET

Typical sail plan for sloop rig.

relation to the boat's course and the wind's direction. (Rope in this sense isn't a nautical word; instead we say *lines*.) The running rigging is usually passed through *blocks,* or small pulleys, which minimize the friction on each line. Each halyard has its own *cleat* on which it is "made fast" when the sail is raised. (You never "tie" a line or halyard; always "make it fast.")

The sails—The sails are possibly the most important parts of a sailboat. They could be compared to a motor or engine in a powerboat. They are what makes the boat go. Without them a sailboat is as useless as a powerboat without its engine. Therefore, before going any further, let's examine a typical sail to become acquainted with its parts and general nomenclature. You can refer to the drawing of the mainsail as you read on.

As you can see, the *mainsail* is essentially triangular in shape, and therefore has three edges and three corners. Its leading edge, that which is attached to the mast, is called the *luff.* Its bottom edge, that which is attached to the boom and which extends at right angles to the mast, is called the *foot.* And the longest, or trailing, edge is referred to as the *leach.* To prevent the leach from either sagging or flapping, depending on the state of the wind, *battens* are inserted in special pockets along it. These battens are narrow, smooth, and thin but fairly stiff slats of wood, aluminum, or plastic. Once inside their pockets, the battens are held secure when the wind fills the sail.

The topmost corner of a triangular sail is its *head;* its trailing corner is called the *clew;* and the lower leading corner, that at the right angle formed by the mast and boom, is the *tack.* To protect against strain, each of these corners has a triangular patch of reinforcing material. For attachment to the lines operating the sail, each of these patches has a *grommet,* or metal eyelet. As you probably suspect by now, each of these grommets has a name too. The one at the head is the *head cringle;* the others are the *tack cringle* and *clew cringle.*

The jib is the smaller, triangle-shaped sail rigged forward of the mainsail. It fits in the area between the mast, jibstay, and deck. Its tack is fastened close to the deck at the jibstay to which the snaphooks or hanks on the jib's luff are attached. Its curvature is controlled by two jib sheets—a port sheet and a starboard sheet—and the placement of the jib-sheet leads.

The *spinnaker* is a sail designed to increase the boat's speed in certain sailing positions and for use in very light airs when a lot of extra sail area is needed to catch what little there is of a breeze. Used in place of or in conjunction with the jib, it is a rather large sail, made of the very lightest of materials (usually nylon), and designed to belly out even in the weaker breezes. To catch any air that may be moving, the spinnaker's lower corner is kept extended by means of a short spar called the *spinnaker pole* or *boom.* Control of the spinnaker's other corner is maintained through a sheet.

As you will remember, a catboat carries but one sail—a mainsail. The sloop has a rig consisting of two or more sails—mainsail and jib and/or spinnaker. Almost all sails today are made of dacron synthetic cloth, which is extremely strong and very hard to stretch out of shape. Dacron also is difficult to soil or stain, resists rot and mildew, and will last for an indefinitely long period of time if properly cared for. (As mentioned before, spinnakers are usually made of nylon.)

When it comes to rigging a boat it's actually a lot easier to do it than to describe what you are doing. Manufacturers frequently furnish complete rigging instructions with their boats, and these instructions should be followed.

When it comes to sails, on a smaller sailcraft put on the mainsail by starting at the gooseneck, feeding the foot of the sail, clew first, into the slot on the boom. The screw pin in the gooseneck slips through the tack of the sail to hold it in place. Draw the foot of the sail out along the boom until the foot is just tight. The *outhaul* (a small rope) should be attached to the fitting on the boom with a

Stepping the mast.

Attaching the sidestays (or shrouds).

Attaching the forestay (or jib-stay). On a small boat this is the only stay that is adjustable and the adjusting is done with a turnbuckle, as shown here.

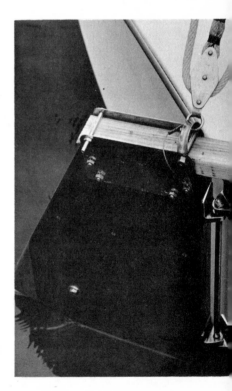

Lowering the centerboard of a small sailboat to provide stability. This should be done when first starting to rig the boat.

The "cleat" knot is used frequently when rigging a boat.

The rudder and tiller assembly is attached to the transom with one long pintle which passes through two gudgeons.

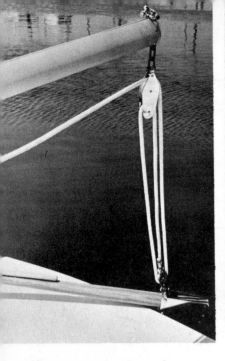

The arrangement of the main-sheet and the rudder varies with the sailboat. This is one of the more common types.

Examining the block (or pulley) attached to the end of the boom. Note that this craft has a tiller extension which some skippers find convenient, particularly when sailing alone in a 16-footer without the aid of a crew.

Attaching the head of the jib sail to the jib halyard.

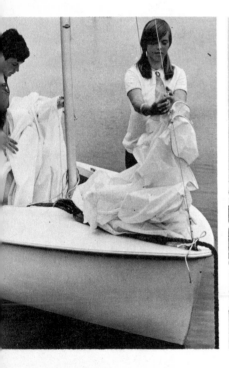

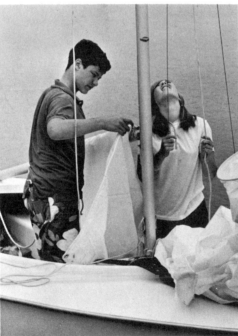

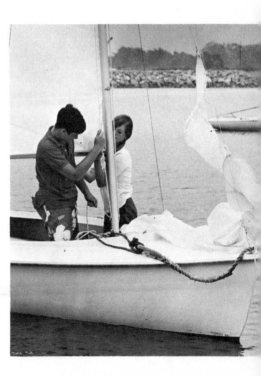

While Pamela attaches the jib to the forestay with so-called "hanks," Trippie "bends" on the mainsail.

Pamela looks aloft to make sure her halyards (ropes or lines which raise the sails) are not crossed.

After Trippie has raised the main-sail with the main halyard, Pamela helps him pull the sail tighter by adjusting the downhaul.

The mainsail goes up first. (Photos courtesy Howey Caufman)

bowline, then passed through the clew of the sail, through the fitting, around again and cleated on the boom. Next, fasten the "jiffy shackle" on the mainsail halyard to the head of the mainsail, and feed the luff of the sail into the mast slot until all the luff is in the slot. Hoist the sail fully and adjust the downhaul (until the luff is tight) and cleat it. If you have a track or slide cleat, you will have to learn through practice how to adjust it properly.

With the mainsail bent on, the battens can be placed in their pockets. (Battens give the leach of the sail its proper shape, and if you fail to use them regularly you run the risk of permanently distorting the sail.) The battens are of various lengths, corresponding to the length of their respective pockets. The shortest pockets and battens are toward the foot and the head; the longer ones are in the middle of the leach. The battens should fit their pockets loosely and they should be tied through the grommets on the sails and through holes in the ends of the battens at the leach. Sometimes the batten pockets have snappers at the outer end to hold in the bat-

tens, and on some of the newer sails there are trick pockets which have no fastening but from which the battens can't blow out. On some of the smaller mainsails the battens are sewn in and are held permanently in place.

To attach the jib, hook the luff to the forestay and shackle the tack to the deck fitting. The jib halyard is then attached to the jib just as the mainsail was. Shackle the "jiffy shackle" on the jib sheets to the clew of the sail and run them aft on either side of the mast, through the sliding blocks, to the jam cleats on the cuddy. The jib is now ready for hoisting.

If the boat has a portable rudder, it has probably been stored ashore; it should now be installed. This can be done simply by sliding the rudder in the pintles (slots or supports used to hold the rudder and allow it to turn freely) on the transom. The tiller is now slipped into its socket at the top of the rudder and under the traveller. Don't try to sail a boat without a tiller, or you'll find that you have no way to control the boat. The tiller controls the boat's steering mechanism, without which you're at the mercy of the wind. Most modern small sailboat rudders are of the kick-up type, which means that they will automatically kick up when in shallow water or when they hit a rock or other obstacle. Be sure that this pivoting rudder is always all the way down each time you set sail. Some rudders sink if you drop them overboard, so be careful.

Before you set sail, be sure to move everything on the boat to see how it works. Raise and lower the centerboard several times. (Until you're more familiar with sailing it's best to keep the centerboard down all the time.) Check your tiller before setting sail, examine the stays, haul the sheets in and out, and the halyards up and down.

When getting underway, hoist the mainsail first, then the jib. The only possible exception to this rule is when taking off downwind; then it may be more convenient to hoist the jib first. In most cases, however, if you should hoist the jib first, the wind may catch it and

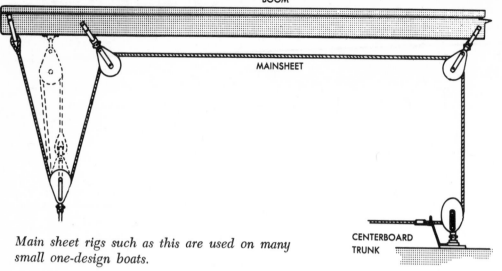

BOOM

MAINSHEET

Rigging guides.

CENTERBOARD
TRUNK

*Main sheet rigs such as this are used on many
small one-design boats.*

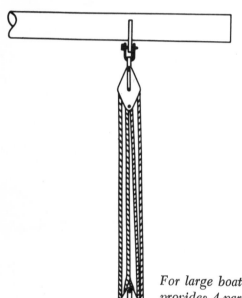

*For large boats with roller reefing gear, this rig
provides 4-part main sheet and a free-swinging
jam cleat with no fittings in the way on deck.*

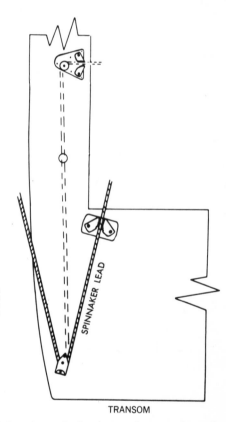

SPINNAKER LEAD

TRANSOM

*Better trimming of the spinnaker results when
leads are passed through a suitable fitting as
far aft and as far outboard as possible.*

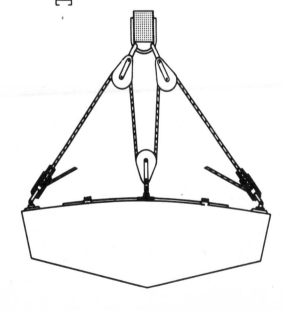

*Typical of small cruising boats, this rig provides
a double-ended main sheet designed to permit
trimming from either side of the boat.*

(*Drawings courtesy Seaboard Marine Supply Company*)

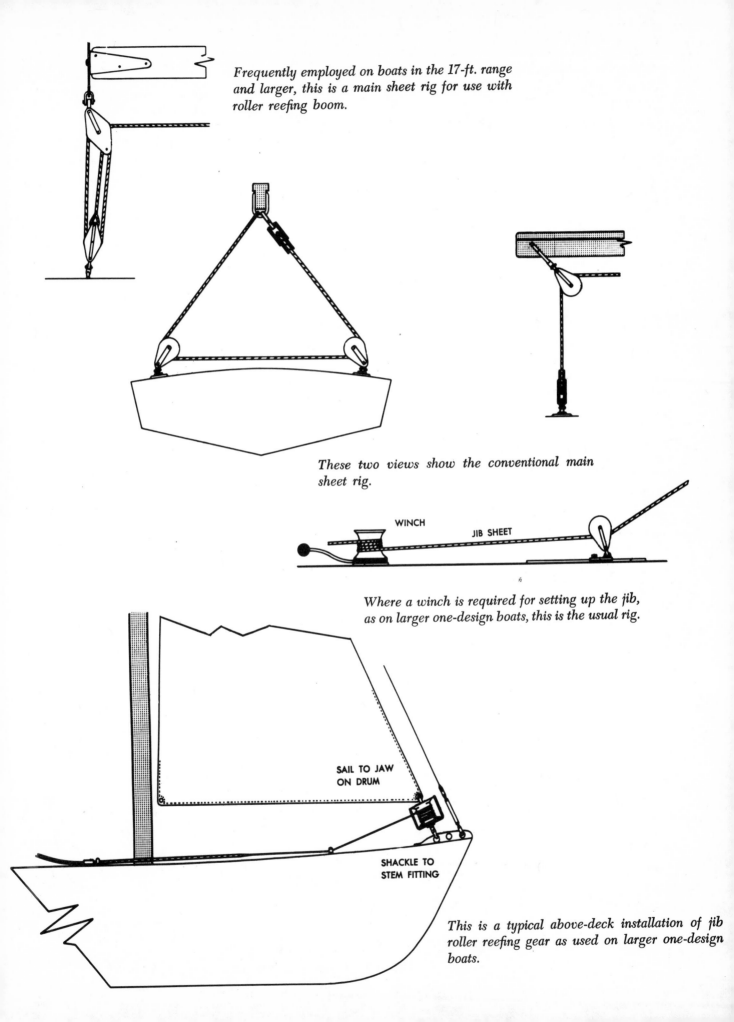

Frequently employed on boats in the 17-ft. range
and larger, this is a main sheet rig for use with
roller reefing boom.

These two views show the conventional main
sheet rig.

WINCH

JIB SHEET

Where a winch is required for setting up the jib,
as on larger one-design boats, this is the usual rig.

SAIL TO JAW
ON DRUM

SHACKLE TO
STEM FITTING

This is a typical above-deck installation of jib
roller reefing gear as used on larger one-design
boats.

carry the bow of the boat away from the wind. But if you hoist the mainsail first, the pressure of the wind on it simply makes you head into the wind so that you won't start before you are ready. (Actually, many sailors don't hoist the jib until they are ready to cast off from their mooring or dock or to raise their anchors.) When hoisting, haul on the halyards until all wrinkles disappear along the luff of the sails. After cleating the halyards make them up into neat coils and place them neatly on the cleats. After the sails are up, they will flap from side to side as the wind strikes them. Watch out for the boom. As the wind shifts slightly, the breeze will blow first on one side of the sail and then on the other, sending the boom swinging from side to side. Slack off on the sheets so that any movement of the sails isn't too restricted until you are ready to get underway.

Once a boat is fully rigged, the next order of business is getting underway. This family in a 24-footer has chosen to leave the harbor under power of the boat's auxiliary motor, a common practice, particularly in crowded or narrow harbors. The mainsail goes up first as the boat moves along slowly under power, then the jib. (This boat carries a Genoa type jib which is larger than the working jib.) The engine is shut off as soon as the sails start to fill with wind. (Photos courtesy Howey Caufman)

5. The Wind and How It Makes a Sailboat Go

It's a lot easier to sail a boat than to try to explain to someone what you are doing. Understandably, the person who wants to learn the art of sailing must have a little idea of the theory. Actually a sailboat can go in any direction except directly into the wind. To sail against the wind, one must tack the boat or angle it into the wind. The points or positions of sailing are governed by wind direction and the trim of the sail (location of the boom). The closer the boat has to sail to the wind the closer the boom is brought to the centerline of the craft. The more the course of the boat approaches a run (wind coming over the stern) the farther the boom is eased off away from the centerline.

It's an over-simplification to say that the pushing effect of the wind on the sail makes the boat go. There are other forces such as the force which is developed by the leeward (away from the wind) side—in other words, some of the wind engages the sail and exerts a pushing force upon it. Other air currents slip past the sail, which creates an area of reduced pressure, or suction, on the other side. This suction pulls the sail forward. (It has been said that this pulling force contributes as much as three-fourths of the driving force when close-hauled.) Both the pushing and pulling forces of the wind combine to make your sail work. While the wind gives the drive to the sail area, the centerboard or keel tends to resist any side pressure, with the result that the boat moves forward.

One of the great mysteries to some people who have never been students of physics is how a sailboat goes toward the wind at all. Basically, it is like a watermelon seed being squeezed between thumb and forefinger. The pressure of the wind on the sail above, and the pressure of the water on keel or centerboard below, are the two forces that squeeze the boat ahead.

The principal function of the second sail, the jib (usually called working jib), besides furnishing additional drive in itself, is to guide the wind around the leeward side of the mainsail. This guidance of the wind is called the *slot effect* and greatly improves the performance and speed of a boat by increasing the suction, or pulling effect.

When running before the wind, push-pull forces are almost exactly opposite to those

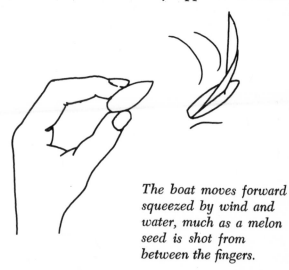

The boat moves forward squeezed by wind and water, much as a melon seed is shot from between the fingers.

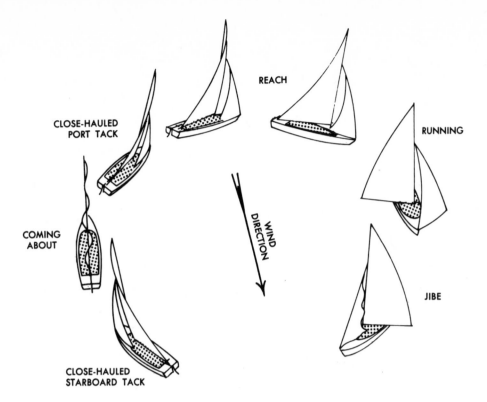

The basic sailing positions or points.

when sailing close-hauled. In other words, the push on the windward side of the sail contributes about three-fourths of the driving force, while the remaining fourth comes from the suction, or pulling effect, on the leeward side. The wind hits the sail nearly broadside, then pushes out in both directions causing a turbulent mass of air that keeps moving ahead of the craft and extending forward from two to six boat lengths. When running or broad-reaching, the working jib has little driving force, since it's blanketed by the mainsail. To supplant the inefficient jib, the spinnaker was invented and perfected for use when running

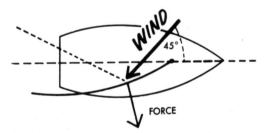

Principle of sailing close to the wind—"beating."

or broad- or beam-reaching. It noticeably increases the speed of the boat because usually it is about double the area of the mainsail and jib.

In sailing, the wind is your only boss. Some people simply have to train themselves to think about and notice the wind and in what direction it is blowing. To others, thinking about and noticing the wind comes naturally.

If you are one of those to whom wind direction is something you must cultivate, form the daily habit of noticing it. Look at the trees, at smoke from chimneys, at smoke from a cigarette, the little ripples on the surface of the water. Feel the breeze in your hair, on the back of your neck. Put your face to the wind and turn it from side to side and you'll hear the wind first in one ear and then the other; when you hear it equally in both ears, your nose is pointed into the wind.

Most experienced sailors use a tell-tale on their boat. You can make one of your own from colored ribbon, a piece of cloth or string, in fact anything that you can tie to the stays of your boat. Some sailors insist on having a

The wind makes its fleeting patterns ("catpaws") in the water around these cruising-type small sailboats. These craft are fitted out with overnight gear. Note the boomtents. (Courtesy Howey Caufman)

pennant at the very head of the mast to show wind direction, but a one-foot tell-tale will tell you almost as much as the mast-top pennant, is much easier to install and is at an eye level when you are sailing your craft, saving you a certain amount of neck-craning. The tell-tales indicate the angle of the apparent wind. The term "apparent wind" is the difference between the true wind and the forward speed of the boat. This is the wind effect you sail with; *if you keep the head of the sail nearly parallel to the tell-tale, you will obtain the maximum drive from the body of the sail.*

You'll find that you'll grow accustomed to checking the tell-tales to indicate the thousands of sometimes almost imperceptible wind shifts that will occur in one afternoon.

Get in the habit of watching the wind on the water. On a calm day, watch the "cat-paws" of wind make their fleeting patterns. On a rough day, watch the dark patches moving across the water; the heavier the wind, you will notice, the darker the color. By keeping a watchful eye on the water to windward, you're ready for whatever blows your way.

For ocean sailing, you must consider the effects of the tide and current in addition to the wind. Tide and current flow in one direction for a given number of hours, and in the next period they flow the opposite way. Unless you sail where the current runs very strong, it's enough to know when the tide is high (flood) and when it is low (ebb) and the direction of the tide. You can usually find tide tables listed in your local newspaper. It's easier, of course, to sail with the tide.

Sailing to windward is usually the wettest, the most challenging, and the most enjoyable part of sailing. As stated previously, a boat can't sail directly into the wind, since the sails won't fill and exert the proper pressure. However, a boat can arrive at a point directly upwind by sailing a close-hauled course at an angle to the wind and permitting the wind to strike the sails a glancing blow. This procedure involves a series of zigzag courses, during which time you're able to sail at approximately 45-degree slants, or tacks, first one way and then another into the wind.

The whole object in windward sailing is to "point" as high (sail as close) to the wind as possible at maximum speed without stopping the boat's way. Therefore, when sailing close-hauled or "on the wind," the sheets should be hauled in hard so that the sails are trimmed as flat as practicable and the boom is as close to the centerline of the boat as advisable. The leech of the sails should not curve to windward. Care must be taken to get the boom in a proper position so that the craft will sail at its maximum speed and not stall. If a boat points too high into the wind, it will slow down and come to a stop because the airfoil of the sail has been broken. This is called *pinching*; if the boom is too close to the center of the boat it may be causing excessive heeling with little forward movement. For this reason it's generally best to have the end of the boom pointing to the lee quarter but not extending over the side of the boat. Once you discover where it should be to make the boat sail best to windward you are well on your way to knowing the fine points of sailing. Just how far the sails should be sheeted, however, depends on how full or how flat the sails are cut, and how much breeze and sea there is.

Some sailboats can't sail any closer than 45 degrees to the true wind direction, while others can sail closer. The best way to determine if you are sailing as close into the wind as possible is to turn the boat gradually up into the wind until the luff of the sail begins to shiver and shake. The jib is generally the first to show signs of pinching; it will flutter at its luff. Then the mainsail will begin to shake at its luff. This indicates that you have sailed too far into the wind so that the wind is now blowing on both sides of the sails. When this occurs, move the tiller away from the sails so that the boat will head farther from the wind. Since the wind is almost continually changing in strength and slightly in direction, it's a good idea to test frequently by pushing the tiller toward the sails and pointing up to make sure you are sailing as close to the wind as possible. By experimenting several times, you'll soon know how far you can point up before the sails begin to flutter or luff.

On boats with fixed keels, nothing further in the form of adjustments is required to sail into the wind. In boats having a centerboard, the board as well as the sheets must be adjusted for the different points of sailing. When going to windward, the centerboard should be lowered all the way to prevent the boat from sliding leeward.

When sailing close into the wind, a boat will achieve its greatest angle of heel or tilt. The helmsman and crew should sit on the windward (high) side of the boat when close-hauling. In this position you and your crew will feel more secure and will act as a live ballast to help balance the boat. If the wind is puffy and the boat heels excessively, the method used to avoid a capsize due to a sudden blast of wind is, as previously described, to release the strain on the mainsail by slacking off its sheet and permitting the sail to swing out freely, thus spilling the wind. Another method is to swing the boat directly into the wind. Sometimes both methods may be used to prevent capsizing. After the puff has passed, you can resume your normal sailing into the wind.

When sailing close-hauled, be sure that you have a firm grip on the tiller. But always move the tiller carefully; never swing it back and forth from side to side. Frequent and quick movement of the tiller will slow down your boat. The way the sails fill, the feel of the wind on your face, or the direction of the tell-tales will dictate small changes in steering. If the boat was properly designed, it will have a slight weather helm of about five degrees. This means that the tiller must be kept pulled toward the windward side. If the tiller is unattended, the boat will turn into the wind and luff. This is a *very* important safety factor.

In an emergency, you can let go of the tiller and slack off both the jib and mainsail sheets. The boat will swing around and lie more or less quietly, pointing up into the wind. To test this, let your tiller ease off to the leeward and immediately your speed should be lowered, the angle of heel should be decreased, and the bow should swing up for a luff. Catch it before it pinches or stops.

As stated previously, a boat can arrive at a point directly upwind only by making a series of diagonal slants, or tacks, first one way, then the other. A boat is on a *port tack* when the bow moves to the starboard and the wind comes over the port bow, port beam, or port quarter. Conversely, a boat is on a *starboard tack* when the bow swings to the port and the wind comes over the starboard bow, starboard beam, or starboard quarter. As you can see, the name of the tack is determined by the direction from which the wind is blowing.

Changing a sailboat's course so that the bow swings past the eye of the wind and onto the other tack is called *coming about*. Assume you are sailing on a port tack. Swing the tiller sharply to starboard (leeward side), or toward the sail, thus causing the bow to turn to port. At the same time, release the jib sheet (the starboard or leeward sheet) so that the jib won't present any resistance to the wind as the bow swings into the eye of the wind. Be careful to ease the mainsail sheet loose so that you don't heel too suddenly. For an instant the boat will be pointed directly into the wind, with the sails shaking violently. As the boat continues to swing around, the wind will strike the sail more fully and the jib must be trimmed. It will fill and push the bow of the boat around to the starboard tack. Midship the rudder as you approach the new heading (a starboard tack), and when straightaway set the sails again. The reverse procedure is followed when swinging from a starboard tack to a port tack.

Be careful when coming about. The boom swings from one side of the boat to the other. If you aren't watching, it can strike you or

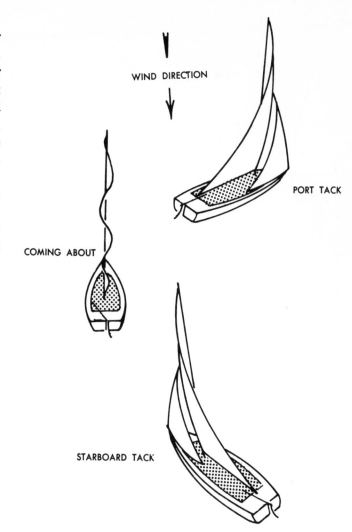

Tacking maneuver in a sloop.

one of your crew members on the head or even knock someone right out of the boat. To prevent this, the command, "Ready about," should be given as a warning to cast-off (uncleat) the jib sheet and to prepare a change from one side of the boat to the other. The command, "Over," or "Hard alee," is given as the tiller is pushed to the lee side of the boat and the bow goes through the eye of the wind; anyone in the way of the boom ducks.

During this operation the crew should gently move to the opposite side of the boat, which now becomes the weather side. Don't come about too fast or too slow. Carried out correctly, coming about will be one smooth, continuous operation and the boat will imme-

These four photos show a "coming about" sequence (changing the position of the boat with the wind coming over the front of the boat). This is called tacking. (Photos courtesy Howey Caufman)

diately gather way on the new tack. If done too slowly or in light winds, your boat may stop head to the wind; this is known as being "in irons" or "in stays." If coming about is accomplished too fast, you may either overshoot the new heading or capsize. Also avoid coming about in the middle of a strong puff of wind, since the results may be the same.

If you are moored at a buoy, and the current is neutral, the bow will lie into the wind. For an example of getting underway, let's say that there are several boats close to your port side, so you decide to go off to starboard—in other words, on a port tack. (A boat is sailing on a port tack when the wind is coming over its port side.) When both sails are hoisted, haul in the port jib sheet, taking up all the slack. Push the clew of the jib to port; the wind will fill the sail and force the bow of the boat to starboard. As soon as the boat begins to swing around, let go of the sail and take up on the starboard jib sheet. Swing the tiller to port; this will help push the nose of the boat to starboard. (Unlike the steering wheel of a car, a tiller is moved in the direction opposite to the one you wish to swing the boat.) Then trim the mainsail by taking in the mainsheet until the sail is fairly flat. As the jib pushes the boat around, the mainsail will fill, and the boat will move forward. At this movement, cast off the mooring or carry it down the port side and you'll begin to make headway. Bring the tiller back to starboard, so that the boat doesn't fall off too much. When the boat is on the desired course, bring the tiller amidships (to the center).

In casting off the mooring line make certain that everything is clear. In the above example, let's assume you go out to your mooring in a dinghy. Your mooring line should be over the starboard bow and your dinghy's painter taken aft and brought around forward on the port side outside all shrouds and stays. Then it should be passed around the bow to the starboard side and secured to the mooring line. By following this procedure you won't have any fouling of lines when casting off.

If your boat should be tailing off in a strong current and the wind blowing from the opposite direction over your stern, you may leave before the wind, using the jib alone until you are clear, with enough way on so that your boat will steer. Then you can luff head to the wind and, with the jib sheets loose, quickly hoist your mainsail and be off on your desired course.

Leaving a dock is easy if the boat is to leeward (on the side away from the wind). First, unfasten the bow and stern lines and then back the jib on the desired side. As the bow swings away from the side of the pier, trim the mainsail until it's at the proper angle and the boat moves ahead. Adjust the course to steer by the tiller, and keep the sheets well in hand. Set your sails close-hauled to get clear. If your boat is on the windward side of the dock, cast off the lines, and give the boat a smart shove to carry it clear while the mainsail is being trimmed. When on the desired course, trim the jib. When leaving a downwind dock, sail out under jib alone, until the boat is sufficiently clear so that you can head into the wind. You can then raise the mainsail.

If you're bottled in by other boats so that you can't maneuver easily, or if the direction of the wind is such that you can't maneuver, the logical solution for the novice is to use an outboard motor or auxiliary power to get into a position where he has maneuvering room. As you become an expert in sailing, you'll be able to get away from situations in which you now require help from others.

When a sailboat is under way and is neither sailing to windward nor before the wind, it is said to be reaching. In other words, the craft sails more or less across the wind. When sailing in this manner, your boat is able to sail from one point to another and return with no complicated maneuvering.

Actually, although a boat is considered to be sailing on a reach when the wind is coming directly from the side of the craft, there are three names given to reaching, depending on the location of the wind. For example, when the wind comes from a point directly abeam, the craft is on a *beam reach*. When the wind comes from a direction between that of a beam reach and a close-haul, the boat is then *close-reaching*. If the wind comes from a position between that of a run and a beam reach, it is abaft the beam and you are then on a *broad reach*.

To change from sailing close-hauled to close-reaching, move the tiller up (toward the wind). Then as the boat's head falls off to leeward, set the sails until both the jib and mainsail start to flutter along the luff. Both sheets are then hauled in until the fluttering stops. The boat will move faster and have less heel than when sailing to windward close-hauled.

When on a broad reach, the same procedure is followed after the craft has been put on its desired course. The sheets are hauled in just enough to stop the fluttering of the sails. The boom is usually kept at a right angle to the wind or the tell-tale. Broad reaching is possibly the easiest maneuver in sailing, since the boat then has its best balance, though some care should be taken to keep the sails at their full drawing angle to the wind.

When sailing on a beam reach, you handle the sails in the same way as when sailing on a broad or a close reach. When the sails are properly set in relation to one another and at the correct angle to the wind, it's the fastest point of sailing for most small craft. On a beam reach the centerboard should be about one-half down; on a close-reach it should be about three-quarters down; and for broad reaching about one-quarter down. The most desired positions will be learned only by experience.

Reaching is the easiest point of sailing and is ideal for the beginner to get the feel of his boat; it enables the boat to be sailed to and fro along a certain course. Always turn into the wind at either end.

When a boat is sailing with the wind directly behind, or one or two degrees on either side of the stern, it is said to be *running*. As the boat is running away from the wind, it seems to lose its power and conditions become

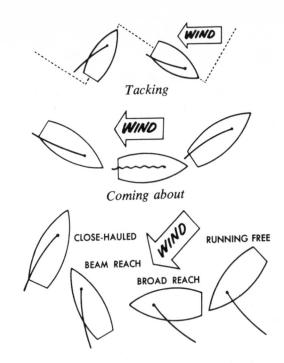

Points of sailing in a catboat rig.

quieter—and this may lull the new skipper into thinking it's easy. Probably more accidents occur on this point of sailing than any other.

In order to obtain maximum power from the wind, the mainsail is set by letting out its sheet until it is approximately 90 degrees (at a right angle) to the centerline of the boat. *Note that we said the mainsail should be at 90 degrees, not the boom.* This is done to obtain full pressure of the wind against the greatest possible sail area.

While *running before the wind* is easy, extreme caution must be observed. If the person at the tiller isn't alert at all times and should allow the boat to alter its course enough to permit the wind to blow behind the sail, there is the very definite danger of the sail being hurled from one side of the craft to the other. An action of this type is called a *jibe* (gybe) and in a case such as this an *accidental jibe*. The velocity reached by the boom during this swing is sufficient to cause a serious bodily injury to anyone unfortunate enough to be caught in its path. It can also cause a great deal of damage to the craft, such as broken rigging, ripped sail, or a broken mast—and it can possibly capsize the boat!

The jib sail does little when sailing before the wind, since it's blanketed by the mainsail. It may hang limp or may bang from one side to the other. While the jib doesn't do the work it was designed for, it does give you the first warning of an accidental jibe. If the jib starts to fill out and pull out on the side opposite the mainsail, you're on the verge of a jibe. To prevent this, give the tiller a quick push toward the mainsail. As you become more experienced in sailing you may wish to try sailing with the mainsail out on one side and the jib on the other (commonly called *wing and wing*) or you may wish to substi-

Method of accomplishing the controlled jibe.

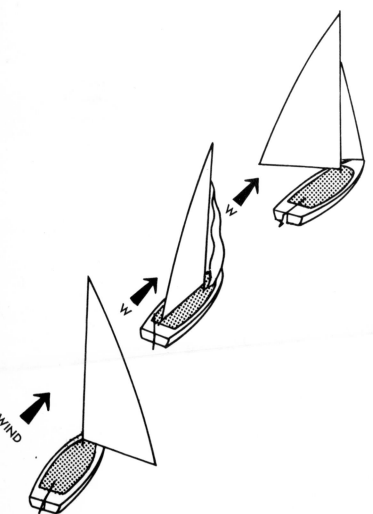

tute a spinnaker for the jib (described later in this chapter).

Before the wind, a boat will move faster with the centerboard completely up. But if the boat shows any tendency to yaw or swing off its course in either direction, it's a good idea to lower the centerboard a quarter of its full depth.

The *controlled jibe* is a much-used maneuver and it is essential to sailing. (Only the accidental or unintentional jibe can cause trouble.) It is generally employed when sailing before the wind and when you have to round a buoy or breakwater where there is limited space, when the wind has shifted and you wish to avoid sailing by the lee, or when you wish to change your course without coming about. Actually, you could say that jibing is the opposite of coming about. In both maneuvers the sail shifts, catching the wind on its other side. The difference is that you come about when you are sailing into the wind, and you jibe when you are sailing with the wind.

Suppose you're sailing with the wind on the port quarter and you want to alter your course. As the wind is behind you and pounding squarely on the sails, you must take care to insure that the mainsail is under complete control at all times during this maneuver. Drop the centerboard while jibing—this makes the boat more stable.

Commence the jibe by trimming in the sheets as rapidly as possible and continuing to haul on the mainsheet until it's almost as tight as when you're tacking. This will reduce the size of the arc through which the boom eventually banks over and will keep the boom from lifting. Release the jib sheet so that the jib swings freely. When the boom gets well inboard, ease the tiller over so that the boat starts turning in the direction you want to go. (The stern will swing into the wind—not the bow, as in coming about.) As soon as the wind is dead astern, ease the mainsheet slightly and push the boom over so it won't swing suddenly, and then let out the main sheet fast. (Sometimes the boom will

These four photos show a jibing sequence (changing the position of the boat with the wind coming from behind or astern). Note how the crew (Pamela) changes her position as the boat changes position. (Photos courtesy Howey Caufman)

snap over fast before you have a chance to ease it over. Therefore, be sure to keep your head low, shift your weight to the opposite side, and avoid getting tangled in the main-sheet.) Push the tiller to midship to absorb the shock of the boom, adjust the jib sheet so that the jib again draws, haul up the center-board, and you'll be on your new course.

Jibing should be practiced at first in the lightest of breezes, since it is a rather difficult maneuver to execute in a strong wind. Since you are following the same course as the waves, there is tremendous drag on the rud-der. This can cause the boat to be unma-neuverable, permitting the next waves that come along to roll the boat over. To prevent this, move all ballast (including you and your crew) as far back as possible to avoid the tendency of the boat to bury its bow and lift the rudder out of the water.

Should you wish to return from a running position to a windward position, it's an easy task to swing the boat, just as you do in tack-ing, by pushing the tiller toward the mainsail. As the craft swings closer to the wind, haul the mainsail and jib sheets in gradually so that the boat doesn't lose its forward motion. It's then only necessary to continue the swing, trim the sails, and lower the centerboard until the desired windward course is reached.

When a boat is in the wind's eye and, having lost all headway, will not go off on either tack, it is said to be *in irons*. To get out of irons you release all sheets and pull up the centerboard. Then sit and wait until the boat slowly swings broadside to the wind. When this occurs, trim the jib first, for this prevents the bow from turning into the wind, and then trim the mainsail and lower the center-board. This method can be slow, and you will have no control of direction. For these rea-sons, it's far better, when you get in irons, to push the tiller and boom away from you and hold them there. The stern will soon swing to one side, the mainsail will fill, and the boat will stop moving backward. At this point pull the tiller toward you and the boat will gain headway on a new tack. This ma-

neuver can be hastened if one of your crew members holds the jib to the side opposite the mainsail. Sometimes in a small boat it's possible to get out of irons by giving the tiller a few quick jerks (to move the stern around) or by taking a few quick strokes with an oar, and the sails will fill again.

When tacking to windward, the duration of a tack may not be the same. Obstructions, channels, sand bars and the like make each of the tacks of different length. (In sailor par-lance, a short tack is called a *short board* or *hitch* and a long tack a *long board* or *hitch*.) All the words in the world couldn't describe the correct length of each tack, for every different condition of the water, the wind, and the ability of the boat to sail close to the eye of the wind will enter into the problem. On long trips in open water, the tacks might be several hours in length. A small boat sailed in restricted waters may have to come about on another tack at intervals of a few minutes. The only rule is to keep a tack as long as pos-sible, for each time you come about reduces the speed of the boat, demands adjusting of sails, and causes the crew to shift from side to side.

When sailing before the wind, the jib isn't overly effective. For this reason, a spinnaker is often substituted when on a beam reach and when running. It's hoisted by a halyard to a sheave or block generally located just above the point where the jib-stay is attached to the mast. On one tack the spinnaker pole is at-tached. (The inboard end of this pole fits into a socket or hooks onto the mast.) The sheet leads from the other tack or clew, out-side the shrouds, under the boom, aft to a block near the stern and back to the cockpit. This permits trimming from the cockpit. A similar sheet, called a guy, is secured where the tack is attached to the spinnaker pole; it leads aft, outside the shrouds on the wind-ward side.

For most smaller boats, "turtles" are used to hold the spinnaker ready for use. A turtle is a bag or bucket into which the spinnaker is folded and it's often left forward on the deck,

Sailing downwind with spinnaker unfurled. (Beckner Photo Service)

Reaching with spinnaker unfurled. (Beckner Photo Service)

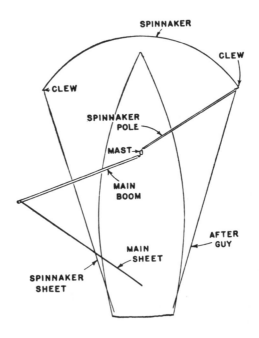

An overhead view of a typical spinnaker arrangement.

with the guy and sheet attached to the sail. This leaves only the halyard and pole to attach, and the sail is ready to hoist. Cartons or boxes are used effectively on smaller craft. The carton is placed on the side deck and the spinnaker hoisted under the lee of the jib.

While the task of setting the spinnaker can be handled by one crew member, it's better for two to do the job. One crew member can set the spinnaker pole while the other can haul on the halyard. To set the pole, move it to the windward side and snap the end over the spinnaker guy. Then fasten the spinnaker lift on the middle of the pole and hook the pole to the mast. Before the pole is set, the spinnaker sheet and guy are slacked and one is secured on each clew of the sail. The halyard is also fastened to the head of the sail.

When this preparation is accomplished, the spinnaker can be raised. The member of the crew who has set the pole hoists the spin-

naker as the boat turns to its new course off the wind. Just as soon as the halyard is cleated, the spinnaker guy is trimmed in order to pull the sail into a drawing position, and to position the pole properly. At the same time the sheet should be trimmed so that the pole and clew of the sail are level. When the spinnaker begins to draw properly, the jib can be lowered, if you desire, and secured; some boats carry their jibs up all of the time.

When you wish to douse the spinnaker, raise the jib if it has been lowered. When you're ready to take in the spinnaker, have one crew member release it from the pole end and guy, let it fly to leeward, and take it in under the main boom via the sheet. The person handling the halyard should watch it come in and slack away just fast enough to keep it out of the water. After some practice, this can be done quite rapidly.

Watching a sailboat pick up a mooring buoy

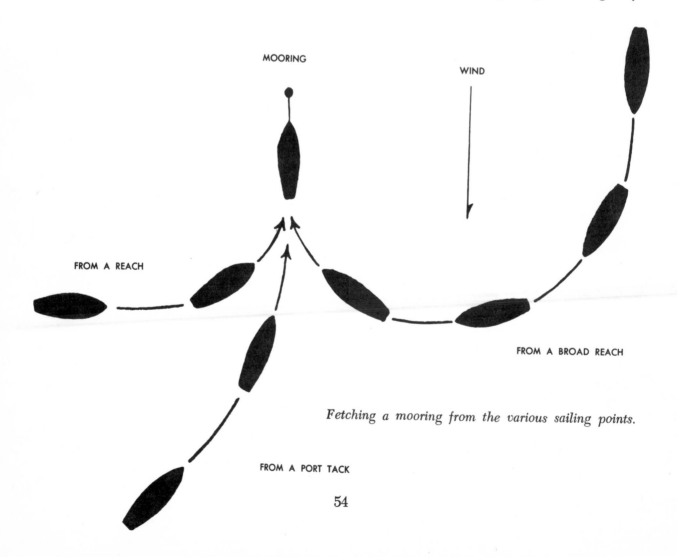

MOORING

WIND

FROM A REACH

FROM A BROAD REACH

FROM A PORT TACK

Fetching a mooring from the various sailing points.

54

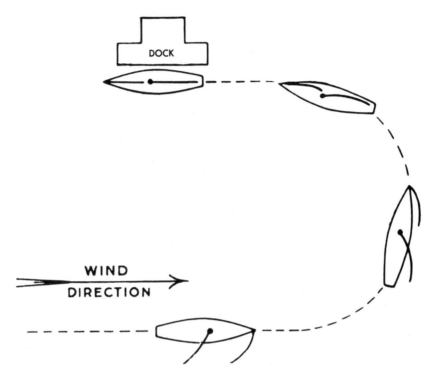

DOCK

WIND
DIRECTION

The best method of coming in to a dock.

efficiently is almost as pleasant as watching one sail close-hauled on a long tack. Making a mooring, or, as it's often called, *fetching a mooring,* is a fairly simple task—that is, if you keep a few principles in mind. For example, except in rare instances in which the influence of the current is stronger than the wind, always come up to the mooring or anchorage with the bow of the boat heading directly into the wind and the sails fluttering. Round up far enough away so that your headway will just carry you to the mooring. This distance will depend on many factors, including momentum, strength of the wind, character of the sea, and so on. Generally, the sharper the turn into the wind, the more effective the luffing or breaking action will be. The rudder can be used as a brake by pushing it hard over to one side and then the other. But remember that when the craft

stops windward, it will eventually be pushed, making sternway. Since most small centerboard boats don't have too great a forward movement when coming up into the wind, a distance of one or two boat lengths in light breezes, or three or four in heavy winds, should be allowed to reach the mooring buoy. Keel boats, because they have more forward movement on them when coming into the wind, usually require a distance about half again as much as allowed for a centerboard boat.

Whenever possible, at some distance from the mooring, it's a good idea to drop the jib sail, unsnap it from the jib halyard, bag it, make the jib halyard fast, and then coil the jib sheets. With the jib sail out of the way, picking up and cleating the mooring is a great deal simpler and easier. Without it, the craft doesn't point as high or go as fast as

This skipper is approaching the dock under sail and has reduced his sail power by letting the jib luff (flap) and is coming in under the mainsail alone for better control. (Courtesy Howey Caufman)

when it is up. Then, too, the helmsman needn't be too concerned about which side of the mooring he brings the bow of the boat to, and the flapping jib won't interfere with the crew member whose task it is to pick up the floating mooring. Also the jib sail will remain clean, since it will be away from the staining drips of the wet mooring and its generally muddy or grimy pennant.

The boat should come to a stop within easy reaching distance of the mooring. A crew member should be stationed forward of the mainsail. From this position he can pick up the mooring by hand or with a boathook, haul it aboard quickly, or attach a mooring line and drop the buoy back into the water. When making fast the mooring line, make

sure it passes through the chocks. If you miss the mooring, bring the boat about and try again. It isn't uncommon to see skippers miss several times before making the mooring.

In coming alongside a dock or another boat, follow the same procedure. Approaching a dock from leeward or windward is simple. If it's leeward, head-reach up to the dock with the sheets loose and attach the docking lines to the dock. A member of the crew should be up forward to see that the bow of the boat doesn't ram the dock. Landing on the windward side, sail downwind until you are beam-on to the dock. Push the tiller hard-over so that the boat swings around into the wind. The hard-over rudder acts as a brake and the boat will be almost dead in the water about a boat length away from the dock. The boat will drift broadside against the dock. Tie up, and the job is done.

If you're coming in too fast to a dock, you can hold or fend your boat off with cushions or fenders, or one of your crew members can do it with his feet; be sure he sits down on the bow and holds both his feet straight out, balancing himself with his hands on the jib-stay. In this way his legs will better take the shock of fending off the boat, yet he won't be pushed overboard.

If you don't have quite enough speed to make a dock, a light line can be heaved to someone on the dock. But be sure that one end of the line is made fast to your boat. If your heaved line misses the dock and you start drifting backward, you can follow the same procedure as when caught in stays or in irons. However, the action of the tiller is reversed. Usually you can get enough momentum to get to the dock; if not, you will have to catch the wind and make a fresh attempt.

If you can't make the mooring or dock by any variety of luffing, you can drop anchor or see if there's a nearby boat to which you can make fast. But if the latter should be your only course of action, take it easy and fend your boat so that you don't cause any damage to either hull. While your dignity

Tying up after a successful docking. Note the fenders that have been put over the side. (Courtesy Howey Caufman)

may suffer a little, you will, at least, be fast to something so that you can stow the sails and beg a tow over to your own mooring or to the dock. If you have an outboard motor or a paddle aboard, of course, you won't have to do any begging.

Before you leave your sailboat, it should be secured. To do this systematically, follow a schedule such as this:

1. Haul the mainsheet in tight and lower the mainsail carefully so that the sail doesn't go overboard and get wet. Release and unfasten the outhaul, unsnap the main halyard. Remove the battens, then the mainsail from the mast and boom tracks. Fold the sail and bag it. If the jib sail wasn't removed on the approach to the mooring, it should be removed before bagging the mainsail.

2. If you have one, slip the boom into the boom crutch. (This is a cross-shaped or Y-crutch structure of wood which is set up to support the free end of the boom in some sailcraft.)

3. Secure the halyards to their cleats, but after fastening be sure that you have allowed some slack for wet-weather tightening.

4. Remove the tiller. If the boat has a portable rudder, unship it, too. Fasten these down inside the cockpit so that they can't slide around, or take them ashore.

5. Coil all lines neatly and evenly. Collect all the life preservers and other gear; either stow them in compartments on the boat or take them ashore. Make fast all loose gear.

6. Pump out any water that has accumulated in the boat. Then sponge out the bilge, clean topsides and deck. Dirt and scum are much easier to remove while still wet.

7. Raise the centerboard (if there is one) all the way up and see that it's secure. In a squally area it is a good idea to leave the centerboard halfway down.

8. Check your boat very carefully and make note of anything or everything that should be done before your next outing. It's better to make any repairs now while they're fresh in your mind than to wait until a later time. Maintenance and repair work are fully discussed in Chapter 12.

9. Many sailboats have cockpit covers. These are canvas coverings that fit over the cockpit, enclosing it completely. If you have one, unroll it and lash it in place securely.

10. Finally, check the mooring line very carefully. Be sure that it runs from the mooring cleat through the bow chock and then to the mooring. If you're tying up at a dock, be sure your boat fenders are down to prevent any damage to the hull. When all these tasks have been accomplished, you're ready to go ashore.

6. So You Want to Buy a Boat

What kind of a boat should you buy? There are now in this country over 600 types of sailcraft between 9 and 50 feet to choose from. This wide choice can be easily narrowed down by obtaining the answers to a few questions, such as: How much do you want to invest? What is the purpose of your sailboat? Do you want the boat to take the family out for a picnic on Sundays? Are you planning to join an existing fleet of boats for racing primarily? Perhaps you would like to explore a variety of waterways, near your home or far away from home. Does overnighting interest you or are you and yours the type who do not choose to camp out? Perhaps you want something large enough to race in ocean regattas. It may be that a large boat primarily designed for cruising is what you have wanted all your life.

One of the things you must bear in mind **is** the limitations of the area you plan to sail in. Take a look at the conditions near where you will be keeping the boat. Is there a strong current in the river everyone sails in? What about dry sailing? (That is, will you be hauling your boat out of the water between sails?) Or will your boat be kept in a slip, or attached to a mooring? What is the availability of these types of accommodations for your boat?

More questions: Who is going to use your boat? Are you buying a boat for the kids only, for yourself and your son? Will your wife be using it and perhaps taking along her friends?

Obviously many factors have to be taken into consideration to be certain that you buy the right boat for your needs.

Let us take a hypothetical family so we can see how these factors fit together.

Our hypothetical family consists of Mom, Dad, Johnny, age 14, and Susy, age 12, and the area their boat will be sailed in is a lake where they have a summer camp. The lake is three miles long and two miles wide.

Here are some factors which have to be considered:

Mom and Dad would like to sail the boat and take along some friends. Johnny and Susy would like to take it out by themselves. This automatically limits the size of this family's first boat. The wind conditions on the lake are moderate, yet shifty and squally. The depth of the water is two feet to fifteen feet. The water is choppy but not like the ocean. The boat will be tied at the dock or moored off the dock, but will be beached at times. The family has $1000 to $1200 in cash and are willing to finance any balance up to $1500 extra they need over a two- to three-year period. A trailer will be used to bring the boat home for repair work and maintenance.

Having analyzed the problem and drawn some general conclusions, this family should buy the following:

1. A 15′ to 16′ boat—children can't handle anything larger safely.

2. Price of fiberglass boat and dacron sails —$1800–$2000.

3. Trailer and equipment—$250.

*The Sprite can be rigged with a single sail as a catboat, or with a mainsail and jib
as a sloop, as here. (Courtesy Norman Fortier)*

Close-hauled 5.5 meter sloops at the start of a race off Newport Harbor, Calif. (Beckner Photo Service)

4. Financing required—$600 at 6% or $72 equals $672 over 24 month or $28 per month. Insurance $50 per year.

5. Minimum beam (width) of 5′6″ to 6′.

6. A bow eye for trailering and mooring on the water.

7. Flotation built into the boat which is enough to keep boat and 4–6 adults afloat in an emergency. Flotation should be in the sides of the boat and under decks.

8. Sail area should be about 125 sq. ft.— 150 ft. at absolute maximum. The kids can't handle properly anything much over 90, so they may have to sail with just the mainsail alone. In light air, of course, everything, all the sails, can be put up but on a squally lake this can be dangerous. Rules should be made and followed for the safety of children sailing the boat alone—life jackets, etc., should be readily available for use. Children should be required to use them at all times.

9. Boats that are organized into classes in the day sailing range are always a safe bet

to buy. The resale value of a sailboat is only as good as the demand of someone else who might want to buy a boat at a few dollars off list. Most fiberglass sailboats lose only the price of the sails (about 10% to 15%) in value the first year. (As a matter of interest, it is almost impossible to buy second-hand fiberglass sailboats with class recognition; there is a standing line a mile long to pick up this type of boat.) Therefore, your investment for one summer of fun might cost you only $100– $150.

10. If your dealer who sells you your boat knows his stuff he is going to look at you as a long-term investment and sell you the right craft. He knows if you take to sailing you will get a bigger boat every couple of years; therefore, to put you in the wrong boat at the outset and squeeze every dollar he can out of you is shortsighted and bad judgment on his part.

If you and some friends of yours want to get together and start a fleet, three boats or more, you usually can get a fleet discount from the dealer. With a small fleet you will have the added fun of impromptu or organized racing.

11. The final effort in your buying the boat of your choice is to try one out if possible. Either your dealer or a friend might just have what you are thinking about. If you haven't sailed too much, don't make the mistake of being the family hero. Take a few lessons if they are available from your boat dealer, and if not, get a friend to check you out. Kids take to sailboats like ducklings to water—they have little fear and immediate responses.

In the last few years, the "small ocean racer," the racing, cruising, day-sailing boats of 18–40 feet, have burst on the U.S. sailing scene in unbelievable numbers. There are several reasons for this:

First, fiberglass construction has brought costs per foot of boats in this size range down drastically (in "real" money, at least, discounting any inflation). Also, fiberglass construction requires less framing and other structural members and these little boats may be surprisingly roomy.

Second, most of the gifted naval architects in this country have given thought to the small ocean racer and have come up with able, comfortable and fast designs.

Third, the economics of boat building and boat ownership are such that while a 50-foot yacht is only twice as long as a 25-footer, only one in, say, 10,000 U.S. families may be inclined to spend the amount necessary for the 50-footer, but one in 10 families find the 25-footer within reach if they want a boat badly enough.

There are several reasons why you might want a boat of this type:

They are generally moderately rigged, stable and easy for two average people to

Racing to windward. (Beckner Photo Service)

This family cruising aboard a 22-footer knows the importance of taking along books and other hobby "gear" to fill idle hours afloat. (Beckner Photo Service)

sail. Many may be sailed single-handed comfortably.

The good ones are able sea boats and one need have no hesitation about taking on some fairly extended cruises.

Often they are trailerable. One can trail to cruising waters quite a distance from the home port and not only have a boat to sail when he gets there but a home to live in and even a place to heat the baby's bottle if that is desirable.

There is good racing available for such boats along the East Coast, Gulf Coast, Great Lakes and West Coast, though not as much yet in inland waters. A few of these designs have developed strong one-design class organizations and have 50 to 100 starters crossing the line in their championship regattas.

These small auxiliaries are often a good solution to the skipper whose family is growing too big for the class boat he's sailing, or for the man who wants to do some cruising as well as racing.

However, one should not be dazzled by the prospect of extended offshore passages in the "28-footer which sleeps six." Six on the 28-footer is OK for an overnight, or when the weather is nice and a couple of guests may sleep on deck. But have you ever spent 48-hours huddled in a small cabin with five others, cold winds and torrents of rain forcing you to keep all hatches buttoned up tight? It's better to stay home.

IN SUMMARY: You'll realize by now I haven't told you what boat to buy. *You* must decide that. But if you answer all the questions we've posed in terms of your own abilities, desires, pocketbook, in terms of the launching and mooring facilities available to you, and in terms of the people who will use the boat, you'll see a pattern emerge.

A happy group who have obviously gotten the most out of their Flying Scot, a 19-footer. (Courtesy Gordon Douglass Boat Co., Inc.)

Double-ended 110's racing close-hauled. (Courtesy Howey Caufman)

7. A Few Things to Know Before Casting Off

Before you take your boat out for the first time, it would be wise to go over the operation of each line and every piece of gear so that you will be sure of its function. This will save you a great deal of time and trouble when you are out on the water.

If you're brand new to sailing and it's a small boat, study the sails, lay them out on the lawn to see what they look like. While they are still laid out, mark their corners for easy handling, so that when you pull the sails out of their bag (your sails should be stored in sail bags) in the cramped quarters of a small boat you can quickly find the corner you want by reading your mark. Lay out the foot of the mainsail and jib roughly parallel on the ground—just as they will appear when set and flying on your boat.

When you buy a complete boat, including the sails, it will usually arrive ready to sail. All that is required is to rig the boat and launch it. In addition to the standard equipment, most boat manufacturers have available such extras as a spinnaker, boom crutch, cockpit cover, outboard motor bracket, oarlocks, and floorboards.

In addition, the following gear should be aboard a boat 20 feet or under and can be considered essential:

OARS—It isn't wise to go for a sail in your boat without at least one oar or paddle to use in case you are becalmed. (If there's wind enough to move the smoke from a cigarette, it will move a sailboat. However, it's possible to

be becalmed, and this is why an oar is important.) One oar can move a 20-foot boat. Remember, too, that an oar can assist you in many ways such as freeing your boat if you should run aground. A paddle, of course, can be substituted for an oar.

HORN or *WHISTLE*—To signal others in case fog rolls in.

LIFE PRESERVERS—Both for your safety and to conform with Coast Guard requirements, you'll want only Coast Guard-approved cushions or jackets aboard. Look for the cloth tag which gives this information. Carry enough for the maximum number of people you expect to have aboard.

TOOLS—Pliers, pocket knife, and screwdriver will have many uses.

BAILING BUCKET or *PUMP*—When you are sailing in a heavy breeze, your boat may take a little water over the side. In a small boat, a sponge or bailing bucket may be enough to bail with, but on a larger boat you'll need a pump. Also when your boat is on a mooring and it rains, you'll find a pump a handy device for getting rid of the rainwater.

ANCHOR—The size and the kind depends on why you want it. If you need an anchor to hold your boat in one place while you fish, the mushroom type anchor will do. A 12-pounder is safe for boats up to 19 feet on calm, protected water free of current or strong winds. If you want to sleep aboard your boat or be away for a few hours, you'll need a patent type anchor such as a Northill, Navy,

Air rollers are a must for small boat handling on shore. This family is getting ready to launch their catamaran. (Courtesy Dorothy Crossley)

or Danforth. An 8-pounder will hold most boats under 14 feet long. The 13-pounder is safe up to 20 feet. The amount of line to be used with your anchor will determine its holding power. For sailboats 20 feet and under, use 100 feet of ⅜-inch nylon rope.

LIGHTS—A search or flash type is always handy to have on board.

EXTRA LINE—Extra line on any sailboat is an absolute must! There may be an occasion when you will need a tow, and the extra line can be used for this purpose. You might also need a painter—a line from the bow ring of your sailboat to be used when you tie up at a dock. Also an extra line can come in very handy if you should experience a "man overboard." The extra line should be of the same size as that used for anchoring.

AIR ROLLERS—A pair of these are indispensable if you trail your boat or beach it.

All of the above equipment can be purchased from your local marine dealer. In addition to this gear, and if storage space aboard permits, the following items may prove useful for the smaller sailboat: an outboard motor; a portable radio to provide the latest weather information; fenders, used to protect the boat's topsides when docking; thermos jug, for drinking water; compass; and foul-weather gear, in case bad weather comes in while you are sailing.

Last but not least—you would not be so foolish as to take your new boat out without making absolutely sure it is insured. Boat insurance policies usually are figured for a specific period of time during which the boat will be in use. Most policies also state specific limits within which the boat will be operated. However, it's possible to sail beyond the state limits by notifying your insurance agent and having your policy properly endorsed. Most boat insurance gives broad protection, including protection against liability for injury to anyone on the owner's boat or any boat he may collide with, against the cost of medical payments for personal injuries, against damage to the owner's boat, and against liability for the injury of anybody hired to work on the boat.

Your author has helped develop specialized sailboat policies which give maximum all-risk protection. Don't buy just any policy; make sure you have all the coverages to give you complete protection.

8. Weather Safety and Aids to Navigation

You would not think of taking off on a short trip in your car into an unknown area without a map. By the same token the wise skipper does not take his boat into unexplored waters without a chart.

Nautical charts are available from the United States Coast and Geodetic Survey Office, Washington 25, D.C., or from one of its local offices, and sometimes can be found at fishing tackle, boat, and map stores.

Nautical charts are amazingly easy to read. On a typical one, every little indentation and point is clearly marked. The contours of hills and such landmarks as church steeples, factory smokestacks, towers, and water tanks are clearly shown for a distance of a mile or so from the waterfront. Each buoy and light is clearly marked in its exact location, and alongside it are its number and type. Dangerous and restricted areas are clearly indicated, with any note of caution that should be observed. The charts give you the exact depth of water, usually at mean low tide, in feet or sometimes in fathoms.

On the surface of the chart is a gridwork of vertical and horizontal lines. The vertical lines are the meridians of longitude, and the horizontal lines are the parallels of latitude. These lines run true north and south and true east and west. The scale of latitude indicated along the vertical edge of the chart can be used as a scale of distance in miles, as well as the scale of miles indicated near the title block. One minute of latitude equals one nautical mile. The horizontal scale (longitude) can't be used to measure distance, as it won't give an accurate reading, except at the equator, because of the way the charts are made.

In addition, compass roses appear at intervals over the chart. The outer rose is aligned with the north and south, east and west gridwork of the chart. This compass rose is used for measuring and laying off a course and bearing referring to true north. Every sailboat that is going to be used for cruising should be equipped with a good marine compass.

When you go out in your sailboat, take a chart with you and check the various buoys, landmarks, and lights. In a short time you'll become as proficient at piloting as if you had been born and raised on local waters, and you'll be able to pilot your craft with absolute safety and confidence.

Without a chart, you should know the signals and buoyance systems on the sea, which might be called seagoing signposts. They are the extensive system of lights, buoys, beacons, and markers called "aids to navigation" which are operated by the Federal government on navigable waters of the United States. At first glance, the system appears rather formidable, and it is—but it can be one of your best friends.

To the sailor who cruises most extensively in sheltered waters and rivers, one of the most important of these guides is buoys. In fair weather or foul, night or day, the boat-

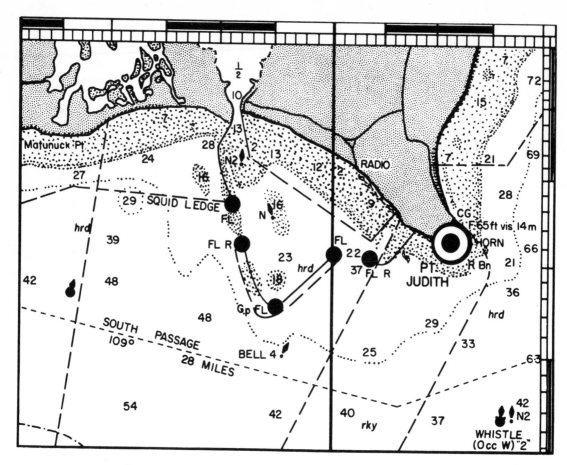

Portion of a typical U.S. Coast and Geodetic Survey chart.

man can use buoys to steer safely through channels and fairways—the avenues of the water—into port. The function of buoys is to warn the mariner of some danger, obstruction, or change in the contour of the bottom. Together with charts—the road maps of the waterways—compass, bearings, and landmarks, buoys are used to keep boats out of dangerous areas and within the proper channel.

The buoyage system has been in use in this country since at least 1767, so it's not something new. At least three distinct methods of identification of buoys are used to reduce confusion and possible error in recognition: shape, color, and number.

Entering a channel from seaward, or a harbor from the main channel, buoys marking the starboard (right) side of the fairway are red and even-numbered consecutively—2, 4, 6, etc. Buoys marking the port (left)

side of the channel are black and odd-numbered—3, 5, 7, etc. Thus, the sailor should stay between the two strings of buoys, keeping red to his right and black to his left, and he should keep to the right side, just as ashore.

Red starboard buoys may be *nun buoys,* shaped like an inverted cone with the top sliced off, or *spar buoys,* which look like a long tapered pole. Black port markers may be either spar or cylindrical *can buoys.*

Numbers of both types increase from seaward. But, remember, if you're heading the opposite way, everything is reversed. Thus, heading out toward sea, right-hand buoys would be black and odd-numbered and left-hand markers would be red and even-numbered, and the numbers would decrease. These buoys mark the curbs of our water avenues.

Afloat, we don't have a white line down the middle of the street, but we do have

68

U.S. Buoyage system: A red nun, a black can, a mid-channel white-and-black buoy, and a red-and-black obstruction buoy.

mid-channel buoys. These are black and white (vertically stripped), and may be of any shape. They'll tell you if you're wandering over into the "oncoming traffic lane."

Buoys are also used to mark obstructions, channel junctions, sunken wrecks, and other areas of special precaution. Junction and obstruction markers are red-and-black (horizontally striped). The top band indicates the best channel. Thus, from seaward, a red top band means that the channel is to the left of the buoy—in other words, keep the buoy off your starboard. A black top band means that the best channel is to the right of the buoy. Some buoys have a white top to enable searchlights to pick them up easily; however, the white color has no significance. Some other types occasionally met by sailors are white anchorage buoys, yellow quarantine buoys, and white buoys with a green top which mark dredging areas.

Bell buoys are generally used to mark channel entrances and obstructions such as hidden rocks, wrecks, and shoal water. These have a metal framework in which bells are mounted. As waves cause such a buoy to rock, the tongue swings back and forth, striking the bell. Some buoys of this type are equipped with whistles or groaners in place of bells.

Lighted and fog-signaling buoys are usually built of an open steel framework, but may be red, black, or stripped just as the others, depending on location. In other words, these physically resemble unlighted channel markers, but at night they show light of various colors and durations. Although they are not spaced as closely together as unlighted buoys, they're near enough to each other so that you can proceed from one to the other with little danger of leaving the channel.

Heading into a strange port, then, we'd first consult our chart to pick the best channel; then we'd use buoys to stay in the channel and we'd follow the numbers into port. Not so confusing, is it? A couple of well-worn memory hints are always helpful. "Right, Red, Returning," and "B.P.O.E." (Black, Port Side, Odd Numbers, Entering from Seaward).

As we pointed out, buoys are maintained by the United States Government. The U.S. Coast Guard does not like to have boatmen tie up to navigational buoys or alter their position or appearance in any way. If you should notice, however, that a buoy has broken loose or isn't where your chart says it should be, get in touch with your local Coast Guard office immediately. You may save another skipper from misfortune.

Local channel markers put out by fishermen and local boatmen usually are wooden stakes, stone monuments, cage structures of wood or metal, reinforced concrete tripods, or even small trees with the leaves still rattling in the breeze. As a rule, unless you know the local waters, it is risky to pass through such a channel. Sometimes the markers are not channel markers at all but indicate fish traps, nets, or setlines. There is no way of telling, so it's best to keep clear.

If you live and will be sailing in an area where there are tides of any consequence you will need to develop the habit of knowing what the tide is doing and what it is going to do.

Various techniques for sailing with and against the tide are mentioned elsewhere in this book. One trick that you might keep in mind is that of lee-bowing. Suppose you are sailing windward and have set your course so as to take the tide on your lee bow; your progress will be fast and your actual course will be closer to the wind than your apparent course. In other words, the tide on your lee pushes your boat to windward. With this in mind, it's often a good idea to attempt to sail to leeward of your objective rather than to windward of it, since the tide will more than compensate your leeway and will carry you up to windward.

The tides and currents of both coasts and the Gulf of Mexico have been studied and diagrammed so that the mariner may use them to help him along his course. Even when stemming an adverse tide or current, certain areas may be found where the current is lighter, or is even coming from astern. Information concerning tides and currents can be found in two publications of the Coast and Geodetic Survey: *The Tide Table* and *Current Tables*.

The Tide Table lists the time and heights of high and low tide for every day of the year at many major reference stations along the coast. The table also lists a multitude of intermediate stations, with differences and constants to apply to the tide at the nearest reference station. Many newspapers also carry tide tables.

The *Current Tables* are used to find the time of high and low slack. They also show the times and velocities of the maximum floor and ebb currents (currents induced by the rising or falling tide). In addition, another section of the *Current Tables* gives "Current Differences and Constant," to be applied in a fashion similar to those in *The Tide Table*.

Weather is probably the most important factor in sailing. It has to be reckoned with constantly. Before going sailing every boat owner should check the weather by radio and, once underway, watch the clouds for weather changes. Here are some of the "tell-tale" weather signs.

Bright blue sky usually means fair weather; but a dark, gloomy blue sky is windy. A vivid red sky at sunset means a fair tomorrow. A vivid red sky at sunrise may mean foul weather that day. There's a great deal of truth in the old proverb: "Red sky at night is the sailor's delight. Red sky in the morning, sailor take warning." Also, a bright yellow sky at sunset presages wind; a pale yellow sky, wet.

The sun offers its "tell-tale" signs. For instance, when the sun comes up out of a gray horizon, chances are good that it will be a fair day ahead. A sunset with diffused and glaring white clouds is a good sign that a storm is on its way. A weak, washed-out-looking sun probably means rain in the near future. The moon gives us help, too. That ring, or corona, around it is a sure sign that a storm is on the way.

Clouds have many shapes and tell nearly as many stories. For example, delicate or soft-looking clouds foretell fine weather, with light or moderate breezes; hard-edged, oily-looking clouds, wind. Generally, the softer the clouds appear, the less wind (but perhaps more rain) may be expected; and the harder, more "greasy," rolled, ragged, or tufted, the stronger the coming wind will prove. High clouds travelling across the sky in the opposite direction from lower clouds mean unsettled weather. Small inky-looking clouds foretell rain; light scud clouds driving across heavy masses indicate rain and wind, but if alone may show wind only.

A thunderstorm can be anticipated by a build-up of cumulo-nimbus clouds, which are dirty gray on the bottom and have anvil-shaped tops. A rapid development of cumulus clouds (these are dense, vertical ones that appear like towers) also will mean a thunderstorm. Cumulus clouds in small, widely separated patches mean fair weather.

After clear, fine weather the first indications in the sky of a coming change are usually the light streaks, wisps, curls, or mottled patches of white, distant clouds which increase, followed by an overcasting of murky vapor that grows into cloudiness. This appearance, more or less watery or oily, is an almost infallible sign that rain or wind will prevail in the immediate future.

The birds tell the fishermen where the schools of fish are and they also frequently predict the weather. When seabirds and gulls fly out early in the day and go far to seaward, fair weather and moderate wind may be expected. When they hang about the land, or over it, or fly inward screaming, expect a strong wind with stormy weather. Also, most birds perch on wires, tree limbs, or any handy resting spot when bad weather is approaching.

Keep in mind that all weather changes are caused by wind. Weather must move to change. If there's no wind, there will be no weather change (and poor sailing). Smoke from the factory stacks or smoke trailing from ships is a help in forecasting weather. Rising smoke indicates fair weather, while smoke streaming downward from stacks is a tell-tale sign of lowering pressure which precedes rain. Remarkable clearness of atmosphere near the horizon, distant objects such as hills unusually visible or raised (by refraction), and what is called "a good hearing day"—these may be mentioned as signs of *wet*, if not wind, to be expected.

By themselves, weather clues have little significance. But put them together and they will generally tell a story—oftentimes a bright and pleasant story, sometimes dull and foreboding. There are also certain broad, general rules for barometer and wind observations. Here are some of them:

1. Wind shifting to the westward, barometer rising: clearing, fair.

2. Rapidly rising barometer: clear and windy.

3. Wind steady, slowing rising barometer: settled weather.

4. Wind in the easterly quadrant, barometer falling: foul weather on the way.

5. Steady, slowly falling barometer: unsettled or wet.

6. Rapidly falling barometer: storm coming.

Check these rules, however, against local experience. For instance, on the Pacific Coast, local westerly winds picking up moisture off the ocean and strengthened by prevailing westerlies often bring rain, while east winds coming off the mountain ranges are more likely to be dry. On the Atlantic Coast, local west winds are usually fair; local east winds, wet and cold. Finally, remember that old Mother Nature being what she is, there are bound to be exceptions to most of the rules.

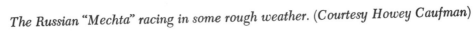

The Russian "Mechta" racing in some rough weather. (Courtesy Howey Caufman)

A good skipper anticipates the movements of those ships or boats which may affect his own boat's course and speed. This comes with knowledge gained through experience, observation, and full understanding of the *Rules of the Road*. These rules are the regulations governing water traffic, and they're the basis upon which maritime law is maintained. They cover all crossings, convergings, and meetings, and they establish which vessel is responsible for keeping clear of another.

According to the Rules of the Road, sailboats have the right-of-way over powerboats, except in the unlikely possibility of a boat under sail overtaking one under power. In this case, the motorboat would have the right-of-way. As a matter of fact, every vessel overtaking any other vessel must keep out of the way of the overtaken one. Also, remember that all vessels must keep out of the way of any vessels fishing with nets or lines or trawls. However, even if you have the right-of-way, don't press your advantage. It can be dangerous! Don't expect all motorboaters to understand your intentions, such as when jibing or coming about in tight areas. In such cases, keep in mind that the only purpose of the Rules of the Road is to prevent collisions, and to do this, they must be mixed with common sense and courtesy.

The rules of right-of-way for sailing craft are determined by direction of the wind and sailing directions of the boats at their time of meeting. The following are the most common situations you will encounter during normal sailing:

1. When both sailboats are running free, with the wind on the same side, the one which is to the windward must keep out of the way of the craft which is to the leeward. In other words, when both sailboats are running free before the wind, the one upwind, which received the wind first, must give away to the other.

2. When both sailboats are running free, with the wind on different sides, the one which has the wind on the port side must keep out of the way of the craft with the wind on the starboard.

3. A sailboat running free before the wind must keep clear of the one that is close-hauled tacking into the wind.

4. A sailboat close-hauled on a port tack, with the wind coming over the port side, must give way to a craft close-hauled on a starboard tack.

5. A sailboat which has the wind aft must keep out of the way of the other craft.

When your sailboat is under auxiliary power, remember that according to law you're operating a motorboat and not a sailboat, and therefore you must follow the motorboat's Rules of the Road, which are as follows:

1. Two motorboats approaching each other should pass port side to port side (give way to the right). In some channels with a current, on the Great Lakes, and on specified rivers, the vessel riding with the current has the right of way over the one going against the current.

2. A motorboat having another boat in her danger zone (from dead ahead to two points abaft the starboard beam) must give way, and shall, if necessary, slow down, alter her course, stop, or reverse direction.

3. Boats coming out of slips into the open, or leaving berths at piers and docks, have no rights until they are entirely clear.

When a powerboat alters course to give way to another vessel, she indicates her movements by signaling with her whistle or horn in the following manner:

One short blast—I am directing my course to starboard.

Two short blasts—I am directing my course to port.

Three short blasts—I am proceeding astern (in reverse).

Four or more blasts—Danger! (Can imply an emergency or indicate inability to understand or comply with signal received.)

If you haven't an auxiliary engine yourself, it is still important for you to know the regulations for motorboats and other mechanically propelled craft, for even if you keep clear of traffic-infested waters, you're sure to meet many cruisers and auxiliary yachts in the course of your travels. It is some-

1

2

3

When two sailboats are running free, with the wind on the same side, the one to windward must keep out of the way of the craft which is to leeward. In other words, the one receiving the wind first must give way to the other. (Photos courtesy Howey Caufman)

times difficult to determine whether a craft under sail has her engine running also, and if you have any doubts about the matter, it will be safer to assume that she is under sail alone, and give way if the steering rules for sailing craft demand it.

There is another rule to which I would call your attention. This states that a vessel which does not have to give way to another shall keep her course and speed, but it must not be taken too literally, as it is only intended to apply when the other vessel fulfills her obligations. There is an overriding rule that states that "nothing in these rules shall exonerate any vessel, or the owner, or the master, or crew thereof, from the consequences of any neglect . . . of any precaution which may be required by the ordinary practice of seamen, or by the special circumstances of the case." If the other vessel fails to give way when she should, you must do all you can to avert a collision; if you don't you may be held to be guilty of contributory negligence.

The boat close-hauled on a port tack (no. 164 with the wind coming over the left side) must give way to the craft close-hauled on a starboard tack (no. 244). (Photos courtesy of Howey Caufman)

9. Water Safety

Small sailcraft have a way of turning over, and the capsize usually occurs when least expected. But if you will consider a capsize as a part of the fun of sailing, you will be completely safe. That is, of course, if you know what to do. Actually, many of the really topnotch racing skippers practice capsizing and then righting their boats.

In normal sailing for fun there is no excuse for tipping over or capsizing—but there are numerous reasons why it occurs. For example, it can be caused by too much wind for the amount of sail carried, by the improper balance of the crew, by jibing in a strong wind with the centerboard up too far, by not keeping the boat under full control at all times, and by being caught in the shifting winds of a squall. If your craft should capsize and throw you into the water, swim to the boat and stay with it. (Most modern sailboats are equipped with flotation chambers so that even a heavy keel craft won't sink.) *Never, under any circumstances, should you or any member of your crew leave the capsized boat.* All too many sailors have given up their lives because they have tried to swim to shore for help, while aid has always come to the capsized boat sooner or later. Remember that a boat is much easier to see than a lone swimmer. Therefore, hang on to your craft at all cost.

To make this task easier, take off your sneakers and all excess clothing. If they are not already on, get to the life preservers and put them on. Even if you and your crew are all good swimmers, the life preservers prevent persons in the water from tiring quickly and will help keep them relatively warm. Even more important, a life preserver allows you to work around the boat without fear. Speaking of your crew, be sure that they are all accounted for and are able to take care of themselves. Occasionally someone may get caught under the sail, become entangled with lines, or get hit on the head with the boom and require assistance.

Under most conditions it's possible to uncapsize or right the boat. But before attempting this, the sails almost always should be brought down and tied to the boom. Start by releasing the main halyard and pulling the mainsail down the mast toward the boat. Then furl it as best you can and secure it with an extra piece of line or the mainsheet. Follow the same procedure for the jib and then make all sheets and halyards fast. Take your time during this operation, since it's a fairly difficult job, especially when your sails are flat in the water. Don't tire yourself out in the water.

Once the sails are down and secured, make sure the centerboard is down as far as possible. Now stand on the far end of the centerboard and take a secure hold of the gunwale or the coaming. While pulling backward, push down with your legs on the centerboard, and the craft shoud slowly right itself. One of the crew members can help by going

Children should wear life jackets at all times. Transferring from the dinghy to the larger craft would be dangerous without them. (Courtesy Howey Caufman)

to the opposite side of the boat, treading water, and giving the shrouds or mast an initial push upward.

Then carefully help one member of the crew to climb into the hull over the stern while the others help to balance the boat and keep it from rolling. The person on board should stay in the center of the craft and bail out the hull as quickly as he can. (Sailboats with low, uncapped centerboard trunks can't be bailed out until the slot is plugged—use shirts or socks to accomplish this—because water will pour up through the opening.) When the hull is buoyant enough to hold the remaining members of the crew, they should get on board and all should begin to bail it out completely.

During the salvaging operation be on constant lookout for passing boats. If one should come near, wave a shirt or shout as loudly as you can. Repeated toots on a foghorn or whistle, or a shirt or jacket tied to the masthead, may also attract attention. Remember that willingness to help in time of distress is characteristic of seagoing folk.

If a boat should take you in tow, it would be best for all members of the crew, except the strongest, to go aboard the rescue vessel. The remaining person on board will act as the helmsman of the sailboat. If, however, the centerboard can be raised completely up, the rudder unshipped, and all the water pumped out, it may be possible for you and your entire crew to go aboard the rescue boat, since your craft will then tow easily without the aid of a helmsman.

One type of accident which can occur in any type of boat is the possibility of a crew member falling or being knocked overboard. If this should happen on your boat and the person doesn't have a lifejacket on, throw him a life preserver, a seat cushion, an oar, or a line, but make sure of your aim if you toss anything made of wood. Even if he's a good swimmer, one of these items will reduce the effort he must put forth to keep afloat, and it will also mark his position. Immediately assign one member of your crew to point at the person with an outstretched arm and to keep pointing while your craft is being maneuvered for the pick-up.

If a person goes overboard while the boat is sailing with the wind abeam or forward of abeam, the quickest way to get back to your man is by jibing. But sail far enough away to avoid coming upon him in the middle of your turning circle. Approach from the leeward side so that if he is in difficulty, the boat

A capsized sailboat being "righted." The young lady first makes sure that the bow is into the wind, and then climbs on the centerboard (daggerboard). Then with one foot (or both) on the centerboard, she pulls the boat toward her and flops it into an upright position. She then climbs aboard, pulls on the mainsheet and sails away. (Photos courtesy Howey Caufman)

For sailboats without a nonskid-type of deck, strips of nonskid tape can help lessen the chances of someone's sliding off the deck. (Courtesy Dorothy Crossley)

won't drift down on top of him. The mainsail sheet should, if at all possible, be trimmed, then eased off to prevent the boom from slamming violently across, possibly injuring someone in the cockpit or damaging your boat's rigging.

If the accident should occur while the craft is sailing before the wind, you have the choice of two maneuvers to execute the pick-up. In the first maneuver, you bring the wind abeam, sail away for a few boat lengths, then bring the craft about and reach back on the other tack and head into the wind. The second procedure is to continue sailing before the wind for a short distance, then tack back. You'll generally reach the person in the water on the second tack. The distance you sail before the wind will depend upon how your boat responds and the condition of the water and the amount of breeze. Through practice and experience in sailing your boat you'll be able to obtain the answer to this question. By the way, it would be very wise

to practice the pick-up maneuvers so that when an accident of this type occurs—which is seldom—you and your crew will know exactly what to do.

Approach the man in the water slowly, spilling the wind from the sail as you go. The sheets should be loose so that the boat is almost dead in the water, and the centerboard should be all the way down during the actual pick-up operation to give your craft full stability. Then throw a line to the person overboard and help him in over the stern. Make the rescued party as warm, dry, and comfortable as possible.

The person who falls overboard should concern himself with three important objectives while in the water. First, *keep calm, don't panic.* Second, *keep clear of the rescuing craft.* Third, *keep afloat the easiest way you can.* If you should go overboard while out by yourself, tread water until you see the boat round into the wind, guess where it will stop dead in the wind, then swim for that point.

If your boat should ever *run aground*, there are specific things that you can do to attempt to free it. Of course, if you are sailing a centerboard boat, you will usually be given ample warning—you'll feel the centerboard strike the bottom. That's always a sign to go about unless you're prepared to take the consequences of running aground.

If your centerboard boat goes aground with its centerboard down, raise it up in its trunk and you may find your boat free. Then head away from the shoal or retrace the course you came. But if your centerboard is up and you go aground, you may be able to free the craft by shifting your weight in the boat or by shifting any heavy gear aboard. If this doesn't work and you're on a hard sandy bottom, you may be able to push the boat off the shoal with an oar. Pole the boat along the path on which it came aground. If this doesn't free it, go overboard, turn the boat around so that it heads in the direction from which you came, and push. When doing the latter, get your back against the transom and push.

78

Don't face the craft and don't push with your hands or chest.

If your boat should get stuck on a soft mud bottom, the problem of freeing it is more difficult. First, you can't as readily go overboard, since you may get stuck in the mud yourself. And, secondly, the oar usually sinks in the mud, and although you may pole the craft a little in the direction you wish to go, you pull it back again when you pull the oar out. In soft mud, however, you can generally free the boat by rocking it from side to side. If rocking doesn't work, the flat side of the oar may come in handy. If you can turn the boat so as to use the oar over the stern, sink it as deep as you can, with the oar's blade perpendicular to the centerline of the craft. Then pull back on the handle of the oar, thus forcing the craft ahead.

If you can't get a keel boat off by any of the methods discussed for centerboard craft, take a halyard overboard and pull it over on its side. If there is some wind, you can add to its heel by trimming the sheets. This method of freeing a keel boat is more effective when your craft is aground on the side of a channel than when you're on an ordinary shoal.

If you should go aground on a rocky bottom, you may have additional trouble—namely, a hole in the hull. In this type of emergency it's usually practical to stuff such a hole with a piece of heavy clothing such as a pair of trousers. This will serve as a check until such time as you can get the boat hauled out and repaired properly. It's sometimes possible to heel the boat to keep the damaged part out of the water.

Safety equipment ready to be taken out by the family dinghy to the larger craft which is being readied for a cruise. (Courtesy Howey Caufman)

10. Etiquette Afloat

Most new sailboat owners want very much to do the "right thing" as skippers when it comes to good manners afloat, and this is creditable indeed. The newcomer to sailing who doesn't observe good manners at sea(or ashore) is soon "found out" and will discover himself low on the popularity poll.

The following are a few common-sense considerations which I'm sure you already practice, but they deserve review:

1. Don't throw garbage or refuse overboard in harbors, or near beaches, or in lakes used for drinking-water supply. (Use shore disposal facilities.) Never throw cans overboard, even in open water, unless punctured at both ends so they'll sink.

2. Do no land at a private dock or float without invitation, except in an emergency. If your boat is berthed in a marina or yacht club, other members have equal rights with you, so don't interfere with their berthing spaces. When visiting another yacht club, pull up to the dock or float and inquire as to where you might moor your boat so that you're certain you don't interfere with some regular member's berth. Then properly moor your craft before going ashore. Avoid tying up across club floats. And when anchoring for a swim, or using the bathing facilities of a club, do so quietly with a minimum of noise.

3. Don't tie up to government buoys, or local navigation markers, except in emergencies. Actually, the law forbids any person to interfere with, remove, *make fast to*, or will-

fully damage any aid to navigation maintained or authorized by the Coast Guard. Violation of this law subjects that person to a fine of up to $500.

4. Pick a place to anchor clear of lines of traffic and outside of narrow channels. If forced to anchor in a narrow channel, take extra precautions should the tide or wind change. It's always best to anchor in an authorized anchorage or to select an anchorage which allows room to swing without fouling other boats already anchored. Always ask permission before picking up a buoy that doesn't belong to you. When sailing in a harbor, never have your tender on too long a line.

5. Know the skin diver's flag and be on the alert when passing dredges where divers may be at work.

6. You, in a sailboat, have the right-of-way over powerboats, but do not abuse this privilege by forcing powerboats into a dangerous situation.

7. Don't run over fishing stakes or buoys, and navigate with care on well-known fishing grounds, keeping well clear of fishing boats.

8. Visiting between boats that are anchored within easy reach of one another is a common practice. But there is a ritual to be observed about visiting. Never board another boat without a definite invitation from the owner. If you aren't acquainted with the skipper, get close enough to his yacht, if you must, and engage him in conversation, but don't attempt to board until he asks you. Never stay

if you're interrupting the work of the boat.

9. Never assume that you are entitled to the privileges of all yacht clubs because you are a member of one. If you desire to use another club's facilities, inquire first of the steward or attendant as to the club rules and regulations. When you're coming in as a guest at a strange sailing club or yacht club, act as a courteous guest. In general, yachtsmen are quiet, gentlemanly folk. They don't call attention to themselves by loudness and rowdiness. Therefore, it's best not to make yourself obnoxious by being demanding, because even if their courtesy gains the upper hand and you are served as you wish, it will mark you for any future use you may wish to make of the facilities offered by that club.

10. Don't pass a boat in distress. Always be on the alert and receptive to possible distress signals. In the case of small boats in distress, it's a good idea to investigate any irregular motion or activity. It is better to know that you haven't passed up someone in trouble. Also, during the summertime most sailing areas are over-populated with young sailors who are new to sailing. Often they may be headed for trouble without knowing it, and it is your duty as a yachtsman to give them a word of advice or a helping hand. Remember that it's a tradition that mariners always go to the aid of those in distress.

11. When you anchor in a small, unfamiliar port, be courteous and friendly to the local people. Remember that their customs and manners are different from the people of a large city by virtue of their isolation.

12. Never drop your anchor on top of another unless there is a good reason for such action. Do not keep your radio or phonograph going late into the night on quiet evenings in crowded harbors.

13. Don't give unasked for advice while a guest on someone else's boat. Pay attention to the wishes of the skipper and never try to interfere with the way in which he handles his craft. Courtesy and common sense are the basis of yachting etiquette. If this is kept in mind, the sailor is well on his way to becoming a true yachtsman.

Young members of a sailing club learn early that there is little room for impatience in this sport. (Courtesy Howey Caufman)

11. A Home for Your Boat

If you own a smaller boat, you don't need to keep it moored in a permanent anchorage during the boating season. With a trailer you can keep your sailboat in your backyard or garage the year around. While the smaller sailboats present few trailering difficulties, some of the larger ones do. For example, most keel-type boats need special trailers to handle the keel, and the boat rides awkwardly high. Besides being able to do your sailing when and where your fancy dictates and as far from your main base of operations as time and money allow, a home-based boat eliminates worry about whether it's being properly looked after, whether it's being used without your permission, whether it has gone adrift or been run down. In your backyard or garage, between trips, you can perform any necessary maintenance jobs. In this way, maintenance costs are reduced to a minimum. Storage, shed rent, and wharfage fees don't concern you. Thus, from the economic standpoint, it doesn't take a trailer very long to pay for itself in dollars and cents. And that isn't taking into account the convenience involved.

Whether you select one of the trailers designed especially for sailboats or one of the standard types, be sure that it will: a) protect your boat from losing shape, b) provide maximum safety and car-riding comfort on the road, c) meet all local and state trailer regulations, and d) permit dry launching and loading with a minimum of physical effort. Either of the two basic types of trailer construction—boom or frame—will do an adequate job. The boom type emphasizes keel support, but includes broad rollers or padded bunkers to distribute hull weight properly. The frame type emphasizes hull support, but includes either roller or channel support for the keel.

When selecting the size of your trailer, the best rule of thumb we know is: If the total weight of your fully-equipped boat is within 100 pounds of the rated capacity of any particular size of trailer, get the next larger size. Next year you may have a different boat and it may be a larger size. Your local marine dealer will help you select the proper size.

Trailering a boat takes some getting used to. Before starting on a long trip, take a few practice spins; see how the trailer handles, and see what effect braking and curves have on your car's handling. Make sure that all equipment aboard rides well without shifting, chafing, or rattling. Trailer balance is another point to consider. Generally the boat's center of gravity should be slightly forward of the trailer wheels so that a sufficient load is carried on the bumper of the car. If too much weight is put in the rear of the boat, the trailer will tend to bob instead of ride smoothly. Weight adjustments will be simple, since a mere shift of weight inside the boat itself will give you the balance you need. Make sure that your boat is secured safely to the trailer and equipped with all safety devices required by law. When taking your trailer from one state to another, check the Motor Vehicle Bureau for trailer regulations. Each state has a different set of rules.

In driving, remember to give yourself plenty of room to brake to a smooth stop. The extra momentum caused by the weight of a loaded boat and trailer means that you need more distance for stopping. Travel a little slower than you normally would, and try braking a few times at various speeds to see how much distance it takes. A rear trailer light, with a brake "flasher," is a must; and directional lights are advisable. If you haven't the latter, roll the window down and use the unmistakable hand signals to warn the driver behind you.

Swing wide when passing and make sure that the road ahead is clear of oncoming vehicles. At crossings, make extra wide turns to clear high curbs after giving a hand signal to warn drivers. Use an outside rear-view mirror, since the boat's bulk will make the inside type impractical, and keep an eye out for pedestrians and jaywalkers who may inadvertently walk into the side of the trailer. In other words, you have to allow another two feet or so at the curb when turning corners and, in passing other vehicles, a good long lead before pulling back into the right-hand lane. Remember, you're driving two vehicles, not one—plus the additional length of the mast.

When launching a sailboat, you should use approved boat-launching ramps whenever possible; they're usually hard-topped and make the job much easier because they're built at the correct angle to the water. If there is no ramp, choose a spot with a gradually sloping shore that's hard enough to give your tires plenty of traction. On sandy beaches or in muddy areas, better traction can sometimes be obtained by deflating your tires slightly. (If you do let air out, remember it before you start your trip home and pull into the first service station to boost your pressure back to normal.) If you have a pair of air-rollers, you won't have to worry about this, since you can leave your car on the road, away from the water, yet launch your boat easily on them without a ramp.

If you're contemplating a trip to strange and distant waters, it's wise to find out ahead of time the available launching facilities. Almost all bodies of water that boast any amount of boat traffic will have a site suitable for small sailboat launching. Boatyards, public parks, and marinas almost always have launching ramps or good beaches. If you are not sure, write for information to the local chamber of commerce in the community you intend to visit. Frequently there is a so-called "Town Landing" which is suitable.

When backing toward the water, come in at a right angle to the shoreline and remember

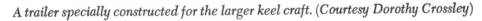

A trailer specially constructed for the larger keel craft. (Courtesy Dorothy Crossley)

Trailers have become so light and easy to handle that lady sailors seem able to manage launching and hauling all by themselves. (Courtesy Howey Caufman)

this tip: If you want the rear of the trailer to go to the right, turn your steering wheel to the left; if you want the trailer to go to the left, turn the wheel to the right. One way to make turning easier is to twist around in the car seat so that you're looking backward over your right shoulder, through the rear window. This places the boat's bow directly in line with your vision, and you "aim" the trailer at the selected point, using the craft's bow as a gunsight. Or you may use a guide to help you back up to the water's edge. Your crew can watch the rear of the trailer as you back and call out instructions to line you up at a right angle to the shore. Back slowly, for obvious reasons.

Before launching the smaller sailboat from the trailer, step the mast in place, attach the rigging, and put on the sails—*but don't hoist them.* Once the boat is floating in the water and the trailer has been removed to a parking area, the boat can be got underway as follows:

1. If the wind is blowing offshore or parallel with the shore, the helmsman should climb aboard while the crew holds the bow. He can install the rudder and insert the tiller, but all the sheets should be left free. The crew should give the boat a good push away from shore and climb aboard while the helmsman balances the boat. The helmsman turns the tiller so that the bow begins to swing in the direction he intends to sail. The sheets are slowly drawn in until the boat stops moving astern. It may be necessary to "back" the jib to make the bow point correctly. As the boat stops and then begins to move ahead, the tiller is reversed, allowing the jib to draw properly, and the centerboard is then lowered approximately half way down.

2. With an onshore wind, the major problem is to get the boat into water deep enough for the rudder to be installed, the centerboard to be lowered completely, and for the boat to go on a tack into deeper water where there's room to leeward for maneuvering. In this case, the crew boards the boat first and stands by with the paddle. As the helmsman climbs aboard over the stern, he gives the boat a push into deeper water away from shore. While the skipper drops the rudder into position and fits the tiller properly, the crew paddles the boat into the wind toward deeper water. When the boat is in water deep enough for the centerboard to be lowered completely and for the rudder to function, the crew can then back the jib so that the bow falls away from the wind on the tack on which the craft is intended to sail. The sheets are pulled in and the boat is gotten underway as fast as possible.

If you have an outboard motor aboard, the problem of leaving a beach is greatly simplified. Just operate the motor until you get into the desired sailing position, kill the motor, and go off under sail power alone.

Most *boatyards* rent lockers and dock space or mooring to customers who use the yard for winter storage as well as to those who use it only for the summer. The activities in a boatyard are usually limited and very informal but generally quite satisfactory. There is a lavatory, there may be showers, and there are usually a couple of rowboats handy for getting to and from your mooring. Boatyards generally offer dockage or moorage at the lowest possible costs. If you don't keep your boat home during the winter and have to pay for winter storage, year-round cost at a boatyard is generally less than anywhere else. Another advantage is that you have repair and maintenance service close at hand if you should ever need it. But, one word of caution: your boatyard isn't likely to permit you to do unlimited work on your boat, nor to bring in outside labor. Have things understood before you store your boat there.

The fastest growing development in the boat world is the *marina*—both the municipally and privately owned variety. The marina is actually a cross between a boatyard and a yacht club, combining many features of each. Marinas generally provide, at nominal cost, a mooring, a dock, a clubhouse with lockers, showers, and other facilities, attendants and watchmen, dinghy service, a marine railway and/or launching ramp or hoist, and many of the other boating comforts of an expensive yacht club. However, select a marina, either public or private, carefully; some are excellent, while others are little more than busy, noisy service stations.

To many beginners, a home for their boat means a *yacht club*. But probably fewer than 10 per cent of American pleasure boats are kept at yacht clubs.

Yacht clubs vary in size, services, activities, and costs. Some are informal groups that pool their resources to buy a patched-up dock and an old shed in which to store gear. They seek new members to reduce individual costs or to get equipment that all can use. Their social events are limited to one a year, usually a dinner-dance at a nearby country club. Then there are the huge, nonprofit organizations with million-dollar properties that include swimming pools, tennis courts, fancy clubhouses, and an endless variety of boating and nonboating activities.

Somewhere in between is the typical American yacht club. It frequently offers group lessons in sailing, swimming, safety, and seamanship to old and young; winter programs on sailing education; dances and dinners; and a summer calendar of races, cruises, and social

Marinas vary as much in size as they do in the services they render. This is one of the largest, at Long Beach, Calif. (Beckner Photo Service)

Yacht clubs range from the large type with membership of several hundred which sponsors dozens of social activities (top) to the modest one-room type with membership of under one hundred. The only social function of the year for the smaller club is a dinner-dance held at a place far from the clubhouse. (Courtesy Dorothy Crossley)

functions. You can judge for yourself how vital to your sailing pleasure such clubs are. But one myth deserves rebuttal: It isn't true that membership in a recognized yacht club automatically gives you the right to use facilities of any other club when you're cruising. Some clubs have exchange visiting privileges, and very few clubs would deny you a vacant mooring in bad weather.

Many yacht clubs have long waiting lists of people who want to join. The number of new clubs has not kept up with the increased number of boats in use, which accounts for the long prospective membership lists.

The greatly increasing interest in sailing, plus the lack of yacht club facilities, has led many sailors into forming their own organizations in which sailing is the prime activity. In many areas local communities have organized sailing programs and clubs. If you like to head up committees you might gather a group of friends and neighbors and start your own sailing club. Often such a group will purchase one or more sailboats and thereby share the initial cost and maintenance. (Fleet purchases earn special discounts.) In one small Connecticut community three young men decided to start a club. A small ad in the local paper told about the boat they wanted to buy and the club they wanted to organize. In less than a year their new club numbered thirty-five members.

For the majority of people an *offshore mooring* is "home" for their boat. When choosing an offshore site, you will want to be sure it is: 1) protected from the wind as much as possible, 2) out of the direct surge of waves from large areas of open water, 3) not in the main channel of a stream or tidal flow, 4) not beneath the mouth of a dry wash, gulley, or feeder stream where flash floods may suddenly form. You should make arrangements for launching and perhaps storing a rowboat or dinghy at a point on shore near where the boat is moored so that you can easily get to and back from it. For this reason it's usually a good idea to moor the boat near a friend's waterfront cottage, a yacht club, marina, boatyard, or public park. In many places mooring spots can be rented for prices ranging from $5 to $50 per season.

In addition to being economical, a mooring offers other advantages. For instance, being offshore, it protects your boat from the dangers of the shore and the attention of trespassers. A moored boat can maneuver better than one that is docked under any condition of wind, tide, and traffic. But the selection of a mooring spot is important. If you're close to the shore or a dock, you'll need only a few strokes of the dinghy's oars to get there. But you run the risk of damage if your neighbors get careless in approaching and leaving their moorings. A remote spot may require more rowing, but—particularly for the newcomer to sailing—the extra space allows greater freedom of movement when leaving the mooring.

A mooring for the smaller sailboat consists of the following four parts: 1) anchor, 2) chain, 3) mooring pennant, 4) mooring buoy. For permanent mooring in most waters, a heavy mushroom anchor is best, but a couple of used engine blocks, if available, can be used. For a sailboat up to 25 feet in length, a 75-pound mushroom anchor is recommended in sheltered areas, while a 125-pounder is best for more exposed areas. Chain (approximately ½ to ⅝ inch in diameter) should be used on a permanent rig, with plenty of scope (scope of at least 2½ times the greatest water depth) to allow for bad weather, which usually brings high water with it. Attach the mooring pennant (a ⅝-inch manila or a ½-inch nylon line) to the end of the chain and then splice it into an eye on the end of the chain with a heavy thimble so it won't chafe through the line. This line should come up to the boat and be made fast to it. Chafing protectors should be placed on the line to protect the hull of your boat. Best buoys are of galvanized iron, fiberglass, or plastic; they can be obtained from your boating supply dealer. Wood lacks buoyancy and soon becomes waterlogged, but a 5- to 20-gallon oil drum, properly cared for, lasts for years, even in salt water. Actually, when making up your mooring it's a good idea to follow local practice or yacht club rules. Marine dealers often make and sell a complete mooring that meets local conditions and approval.

RECOMMENDATIONS FOR PERMANENT MOORING FOR WIND VELOCITIES UP TO 75 MPH

Over-all Sailboat Length in Feet	Mushroom Anchor (min. wt. in lbs.)	Chain		Length in ft. (min.)	Mooring Line		Total Scope in Ft. (chocks to mushroom)
		Length (ft.)	Diameter (in.)		Diameter in. (if manila)	Diameter in. (if nylon)	
Up to 25	150	30	¾	40	1	⅞	70
25 to 35	250	30	1	40	1¼	1	70
35 to 45	350	40	1	40	1½	1¾	80

This group is enjoying a picnic ashore after mooring their craft offshore. (Courtesy Dorothy Crossley)

12. Care of Your Sailboat

Sailboat maintenance is a year-round job. Care of your boat during the sailing season is just as important as spring fitting-out maintenance.

One thing that all sailors discover altogether too soon when the racing season rolls around is that if the bottom of their boat is covered with dirt and slime it slows the boat down. Despite the improvements in hull materials and bottom paints and the stepping up of their anti-fouling properties, the formation of slime and marine growths still constitutes a problem that all sailboat owners (small or large craft) must face. The most effective means of overcoming this is to haul the craft out occasionally (about once a month or every six weeks) and scrub the bottom. To make the slime removal task easier, use a stiff brush, fresh water, and strong soap or detergent. A high gloss on your fiberglass hull can be achieved with the use of a good paste or liquid wax at the time of cleaning.

During the sailing season you should routinely check all rope and wire splices, spinnaker halyard, spinnaker guys, main and jib sheets. All wire rigging should be examined for broken strands and fatigue, especially where the wire passes over sheaves. If the strands fly out when the wire is bent, the wire probably needs replacing. If it looks rusty, it may not require replacing at once but should be inspected frequently. The rigging and the wire halyards should be run through a greasy rag occasionally, but not too much or the grease will be transferred to the sails. Wire rope can also be protected by finishing it with aluminum paint that has been thinned with turpentine and linseed oil. The linseed oil penetrates to lubricate the rope internally. Oil all blocks and winches occasionally to insure that the sheets run freely.

Many small sailboats have safety or air tanks in the bow and stern. These tanks should be checked from time to time during the sailing season by removing the thermos-bottle type plugs to drain out any water that may have accumulated from condensation.

A well-cared-for hull will probably draw more attention than a well-maintained set of sails, but good sail care pays off in other ways—maximum efficiency and substantially longer-lasting performance for small cost in terms of money and time.

Dacron sails require very little care, but never let oil or grease get on them. If this should occur, however, remove spots with carbon tetrachloride cleaning fluids. Two things to avoid with dacron sails are extreme heat (like lighted cigarettes) and sharp creases.

It is suggested that before you put dacron sails away for any period of time, you wash them in fresh water and put them out to dry. After the sails have dried, fold them so that their shape is maintained. Make long folds, roll neatly with as few creases as possible, and put the rolled sails into their sail bags. Suspend the bags from attic beams or in a locker by means of a heavy wire to keep the rodents (rats) off. Don't store where the sun can reach them.

Examine your sails regularly for small rips or burst seams; if you find any, immediate mending will save much more extensive repair work at a later date. This is another excellent example of the proverbial ounce of prevention being worth many dollars of cure; small tears or rips can be whipped into giant ones on a real blustery day. A sail-mending kit which contains needle, twine, and waterproof tape is a useful item for any sailboat owner to have available. For "at sea" repairs, it's a good idea to keep plenty of adhesive tape on board to hold any rips or burst seams until you can repair them permanently ashore.

When it comes to the fiberglass hull, one of its major benefits is the elimination of maintenance chores required by other materials. There are three relatively easy maintenance rules to follow to keep your hull looking like new:

1. Each season buff and wax the exterior of the boat.

2. Touch up and patch scratches, scars and small breaks.

3. Repair any major breaks as soon as possible, to avoid additional damage to the hull or decks.

Most fiberglass boats are manufactured of two "layers" of material, permanently bonded together by chemical action. The outside surface is formed by a colored gel coat. This is a special resin material containing concentrated color. It provides a smooth, finished surface.

The second "layer" is made up of polyester resin reinforced with laminations of fiberglass mat, cloth, or woven roving. Both the gel coat and polyester resin are "cured" by a chemical catalyst which causes them to form a hard, strong mass that is highly resistant to impact and damage.

When buffing the hull to restore its finish, care should be taken not to cut through the gel coat surface. This is especially true on corners and edges of the hull. A power buffer may be used or the work done by hand, using a lightly abrasive rubbing compound such as Mirro Glaze No. 1 for power buffers or Dupont No. 7 for handbuffing. Any high-quality paste wax may be applied after buffing.

It's a simple matter to repair a bad spot with a repair kit for fiberglass hulls available at local marine dealers or through the manufacturer of your boat. These kits contain all the necessary repair materials such as the fiberglass mat and cloth, the polyester resin, color pigment, and complete instructions on how to use these substances to fix any type of break or hole. If the manufacturer's directions are followed to the letter, the patched area will be as strong as the original construction.

Kits for touchup and surface repairs and gouges come complete with instructions.

Injuries to the surface of your hull are of two types: 1) damage to the gel coat colored outer surface, and 2) holes or gouges that are deep enough to penetrate the fiberglass reinforced area of the boat. The repair operations are similar.

For damage to the gel coat surface, you will need a small can of gel coat, of the same color as your boat, and a small amount of catalyst. For deeper holes or gouges ($\frac{1}{8}''$ or more) you will also need some short strands of fiberglass which can be trimmed from fiberglass mat or purchased in the form of "milled fibers." These materials can be purchased from your dealer.

1. Be sure the area around the damage is wiped clean and dry. Remove any wax or oil from the inside of the hole or scratch.

2. Using a power drill with a burr attachment, roughen the bottom and sides of the damaged area and feather the edge surrounding the scratch or gouge. Do not "undercut" this edge. (If the scratch or hole is shallow and penetrates only the color gel coat, skip to step no. 8.)

3. Into a jar lid or on a piece of cardboard, pour a small amount of gel coat . . . just enough to fill the area being worked on. Mix

an equal amount of milled fibers with this gel coat, using a putty knife or small flat stick. Then add two drops of catalyst, using an eyedropper for accurate measurement. For a half-dollar-size pile of gel coat, this amount of catalyst will give you 15 to 20 minutes working time before it begins to "gel." Carefully cut the catalyst into the gel coat and mix thoroughly.

4. Work this mixture of gel coat, fibers and catalyst into the damaged area, using the sharp point of a putty knife or knife blade to press it into the bottom of the hole and to puncture any air bubble which may occur. Fill the scratch or hole above the surrounding undamaged area about 1/16".

5. Lay a piece of cellophane or waxed paper over the repair to cut off the air and start the "cure."

6. After 10 or 15 minutes the patch will be partially cured. When it feels rubbery to the touch, remove the cellophane and trim flush with the surface, using a sharp razor blade or knife. Replace the cellophane and allow to cure completely (30 minutes to an hour). The patch will shrink slightly below the surface as it cures.

7. Again use the electric drill with burr attachment to rough up the bottom and edges of the hole. *Feather hole* into surrounding gel coat, do *not* undercut.

8. Pour out a small amount of gel coat into a jar lid or on cardboard. Add a drop or two of catalyst and mix thoroughly, using a cutting motion rather than stirring. Use no fibers.

9. Using your finger tips or the tip of a putty knife, fill the hole about 1/16" above the surrounding surface with the gel coat mixture.

10. Lay a piece of cellophane over the patch to start the curing process. Repeat step 6, trimming patch when partially cured.

11. Immediately after trimming, place another small amount of gel coat on one edge of the patch and cover with cellophane. Then, using a rubber squeegee or back of the razor blade, squeegee level with area surrounding the patch. Leave cellophane on patch for 1

Steps 1 and 2.

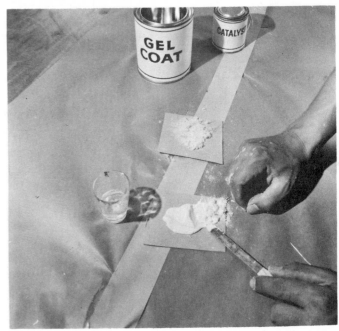

Step 3.

Step 4.

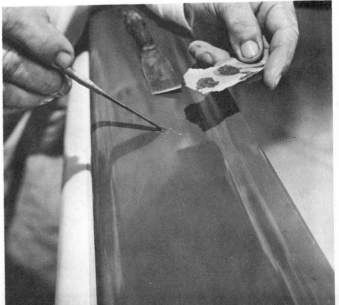

91

Step 5.

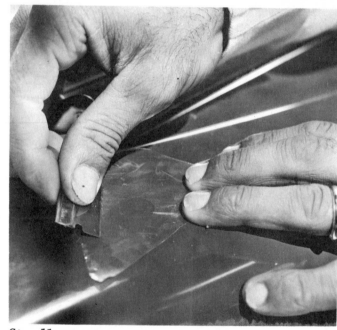

Step 10.

Step 6.

Steps 7, 8, and 9.

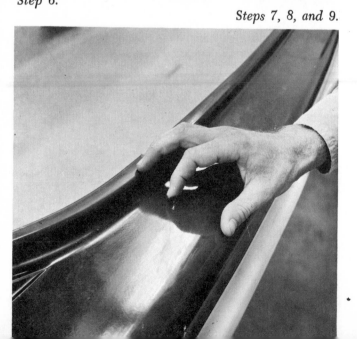

Step 11.

Step 12. (Photos courtesy of Ferro Corp.)

to 2 hours, or overnight, for a complete cure.

12. Using a sanding block, sand the patched area with 600-grit *wet* sandpaper. Finish by rubbing or buffing with a fine rubbing compound. Some slight color difference may be observed. Weathering will blend touchup, if properly applied.

For the average sailboat owner in the North, the sailing season ends during the latter part of September or early October. But you can take some of the edge off that season-end letdown if you'll think of your lay-up activity as getting ready for another brand new sailing season. Come spring, you'll be back in the water faster and in better shape if you're smart about your winter storage preparation.

Storage of a boat ashore can be at one of two places: a boatyard or at home. If you decide on the former, all the problems of hauling out, storage, and some portion of the maintenance will be taken care of by the boatyard. But boat storage costs at one of these places, especially under cover, can be quite high. A large percentage of small sailboat owners and some not so small undertake the winter lay-up task at home. If home storage is appropriate for you, the major problem quite frequently is to get the boat out of the water and to your home. With a trailer, of course, this problem is easily solved. If you don't have a trailer, see if you can find a trucker who will haul the boat to your house or other location. Most of our boating communities have people or concerns who do this work.

When you store your boat, make sure that the method used won't alter its shape. If you have a trailer, it can be stored right on it. However, as you'll probably (and rightly) block up the trailer to take the weight off the tires and springs, be sure that the boat's weight is evenly distributed on the trailer. Often you can help by giving the bow and stern additional support.

If you don't have a trailer, you can build your own storage or use the shipping cradle that came with the boat. If your boat isn't too big, you can store it upside down across a pair of sawhorses, with the support placed about one-third of the distance in from the bow and one-third of the distance in from the transom. If you store the boat in a right-side-up position, on sawhorses, be sure that you cut notches in the sawhorses or use shoring blocks so that the boat is supported by its bottom and not by the keel, because the latter would be an unnatural position. To protect the hull's outer surface, use strips of old tire-tube rubber as cradle padding.

Small sailboat owners can remove the mast and boom from the boat and store them for the winter in a dry place such as a garage or attic. The standing rigging should be handled in the same way. When removing it, coil each piece and tag it for easy identification in the spring. Give the running rigging the same treatment and store them both in a dry place. The sails should be stored as previously described.

To prevent corrosion or blemishing of metal surfaces, apply a protective coating of light grease, oil, wax, or film-leaving polish to cleats, chocks, etc. Wrapping chrome-plated accessories with a cloth or fitting them with drawstring-fastened canvas hoods is generally sufficient winterization. For aluminum, use a detergent-free liquid household wax or a non-acid, non-abrasive, film-leaving metal polish. Stainless steel items should be given a film coat of grease or S.A.E. 30 oil.

The centerboard can be removed from its trunk for a thorough cleaning. Scrape loose dirt from the inside of the centerboard by using steel wool on the end of a stiff wire. The centerboard itself can be stored flat or suspended from a rafter in a cool place that isn't exposed to sunlight. Many a good centerboard has been spoiled from warping and drying out during lay-up. In centerboard boats that have a lever to raise and lower the board, it is best to leave the board in place during the winter and block the centerboard slot.

After the boat has been completely stripped, clean the hull both inside and out

The fiberglass hull is built in layers over a wood form. Color is molded in.
(Beckner Photo Service)

by scrubbing down with a detergent and rinsing the surfaces with clean water. If the interior of your fiberglass boat gets scuffed up a little, you can spray it with a "speckled" paint made for that purpose, available at your hardware store. After you finish the cleaning job, remove the plugs in the safety or air tanks in the bow and stern of your sailboat. But don't forget where you stored them because you'll need them next spring.

If you are going to store your small boat outdoors, situate it three or four feet off the ground, preferably in the *lee* of a building where the snow won't pile up into drifts. Cover the boat with a watertight tarpaulin or heavy roofing paper and then lash the covering securely in place. Several times during the winter check the covering to be sure it is secure.

You can get your boat into the water each spring earlier if you do in the fall what you customarily do in the spring.

Occasionally fiberglass needs painting for anti-fouling bottom protection if boats are left in salt water and some fresh-water areas for the entire boating season. Fiberglass hulls kept out of the water—those kept in the backyard or garage when not in use—don't require anti-fouling protection, regardless of where they are sailed. Painting is also important for

the over-all appearance of the boat; it performs the important functions of: 1) hiding streaked or faded colors, 2) masking scratches, dents, and repairs, 3) smoothing rough texture, 4) providing a smart new appearance and color change.

Before painting the fiberglass, wash down the hull thoroughly. When the surfaces are dry, sand them briskly with a No. 3/0 garnet or aluminum oxide paper to insure a good bond for the first coat of paint. Then wipe the entire surface with a clean rag dampened with turpentine.

To obtain the smoothest possible surface, apply one or two coats of a good marine plastic primer or fiberglass surfacer. This is a fast-drying material and should be sanded before it reaches its ultimate hardness. It is most satisfactory to sand within four to six hours after application. Allow the final primer coat to dry for 24 hours, sand lightly with very fine paper, and then apply one or two coats of a good marine paint, following the manufacturer's directions.

For the bottom area, you may want to follow one of these procedures:

On sailboats that are kept out of the water most of the time, you'll find a racing bottom paint very suitable. (It should be pointed out that this finish isn't anti-fouling—it doesn't prevent the attachment of fouling organisms such as annelids, algae, mussels, filamentous bryozoa, barnacles, etc.) Actually, a fiberglass hull doesn't need painting unless you want to change its color. If you do apply a racing bottom finish, be sure to follow the manufacturer's recommendations thoroughly.

For boats that remain in the water the year round, some type of anti-fouling bottom paint is generally a "must." Check with your local marine dealer as to which is best in your area or for the waters you plan to sail, and follow the paint manufacturer's instructions when applying.

Before installing your spars (mast and boom), clean them with a detergent and wax them with a good paste wax. While doing this, inspect the sail tracks for pulled fastenings. If you find any, retighten them. Wood parts such as centerboard, tiller, and rudder may be refinished, if needed, with either a good marine paint or spar varnish. Follow the paint manufacturer's instructions to the letter.

Also on smaller craft be sure to replace the safety plugs in the air tanks in the bow and stern.

Whether at a mooring or sailing out on the water, the motion of a boat is constantly working the rigging. This causes wear of the basic item that keeps the rig in operating condition —the pins. There are pins at the ends of standing rigging lines, centerboard pins, sheave pins, and cotter pins. Check them before putting the boat back into the water and replace any that show any distortion or reduction in diameter.

The wire-line running and standing rigging must be inspected carefully for broken strands. Check for this especially where the line enters a swayed terminal or at splices. Manila lines should be twisted open against the lay of the strands for a look inside. Broken internal strands and discoloration are an indication of reduction of strength and rot. Lines of synthetic materials usually show signs of wear on the outside, quite apparent to the eye. Any doubtful lines should always be replaced immediately, as renewal is very cheap compared to trouble that can follow a snapped sheet or halyard.

Before putting your boat in the water, go over your ground tackle (permanent mooring and anchor gear) and remove any rust from anchors. Also paint your mooring buoy. Go over every inch of anchor lines, and replace if interior looks bad or there are chafed spots. Check the fastening of the inboard end of the chain or line. Stretch out and inspect dock lines.

After a day's sailing the boat should be left in tip-top condition. (Beckner Photo Service)